Walker Percy

Twayne's United States Authors Series

Warren French, Editor

Indiana University, Indianapolis

TUSAS 449

WALKER PERCY
(1916–   ) .
Photograph courtesy of Rhoda K. Faust
Maple Street Book Shop, New Orleans

Walker Percy

By Jac Tharpe

University of Southern Mississippi

Twayne Publishers • Boston

Walker Percy

Jac Tharpe

Copyright © 1983 by G. K. Hall & Company
All Rights Reserved
Published by Twayne Publishers
A Division of G. K. Hall & Company
70 Lincoln Street
Boston, Massachusetts 02111

Book Production by Marne B. Sultz

Book Design by Barbara Anderson

Printed on permanent/durable acid-free
paper and bound in the United States of
America.

**Library of Congress Cataloging in
Publication Data**

Tharpe, Jac.
  Walker Percy.

  (Twayne's United States authors series ; TUSAS 449)
  Bibliography: p. 132
  Includes index.
  1. Percy, Walker, 1916–
—Criticism and interpretation.
  I. Title.   II. Series.
PS3566.E6912Z86 1983   813'.54   83–4309
ISBN 0-8057-7389-4

Mother
(1899–1982)

Contents

About the Author

Jac Tharpe is Honors Professor of English at the University of Southern Mississippi at Hattiesburg. His doctorate is in comparative literature with emphasis on American literature. His publications include collections of essays on Robert Frost and Tennessee Williams as well as Walker Percy and Elvis Presley. Southern Illinois University Press published his books on Nathaniel Hawthorne and John Barth. He is now at work on recent Southern fiction.

Preface

Walker Percy's first novel, *The Moviegoer,* won the National Book Award in 1962, and misinterpretation of his work began at that time. The citation (printed opposite the title page in the novel) reads: *"The Moviegoer,* an intimation rather than a statement of mortality and the inevitability of that condition, is a truthful novel with shocks of recognition and spasms of nostalgia for every—or nearly every—American. Mr. Percy, with compassion and without sentimentality or the mannerisms of the clinic, examines the delusions and hallucinations and the daydreams and the dreads that afflict those who abstain from the customary ways of making do." It reads well, especially in the last half, but not clearly.

Why, for example, make that reservation between the dashes, particularly since it only emphasizes what Percy makes clear in Binx's choices—that he somewhat puritanically sets himself aside from the world and thus from every—or nearly every—American? And why concentrate on spasms of nostalgia, as if that would help? Even shocks of recognition may not accomplish anything beyond giving aesthetic pleasure. And the intimation and inevitability of mortality may apply if the reader ignores or misreads the epilogue, with its promise of the life to come.

Attacking the citation means little, of course. Yet, actually, the citation probably derives from a misapprehension of the author's intent in *The Moviegoer* and probably represents the kind of misapprehension that led to adverse criticism of his later novels.

Binx was a truthful rebel. So in a firm and sturdy sense he speaks directly. But to very few: Percy himself says in an interview with John Carr that if his characters had to work every day for a living they would not have time to speculate on these matters of right conduct and alienation. Presumably he does not mean that quite the way it sounds, as the saying goes, does not mean that ethics and religion are unimportant for ordinary working men and women. But the remark points up what is obvious—that Binx really speaks only to and for those intellectuals of various ages who found the "hero's" withdrawal appealing and who were not quite aware that Binx was no rebel of the sixties, no flower child, but a rebel of the fifties. And among those he spoke to were the romantics, from whom he expected little, people more or less like his father, because they throve on being outcasts passively rejected by society, while Binx had in fact rejected the immorality and complacency that became widespread as technology made daily living easier and left leisure for boredom and consequent indulgence. Living was no longer fun. People like Binx said nothing about the supposed crimes of America at war and thought nothing about drug abuse, two of the important issues of the sixties. And Percy complicates matters by having Binx somewhat romantically indulge his own desires before he "gets religion," when a conviction of his despair turns him away from fornication to God.

Though Binx says little about ideals, men like him were alienated because they lived in a world recently occupied with what was called a war for individual rights when there were no individuals anymore, that vanishing breed now somewhat analogous to Edwin Arlington Robinson's millers. Advertising marketed all the necessities and most of the luxuries of life nationwide. Even ideas were available by the package, Japanese and Indian imports, Hindu and Buddhist religions, and such French products as existentialism. The result was not diversity but increased ways to conform, especially when everyone got the latest from abroad, Haiku, Bonzai, the Kama Sutra, Kierkegaard, especially Sartre.

The most important misapprehension of *The Moviegoer* was the failure to see that the novel was by a Roman Catholic novelist writing about immorality. Members of the award committee probably did not consider it a theological or religious novel. It seemed far more like a combination of *Nausea* and *The Stranger,* evocations about "making do" that were no doubt the source of its appeal for some readers. Some of the best discussion of Percy's work follows his lead in considering him an existentialist and phenomenologist in his attempts to portray real people in a real physical world without merely being realistic, as William Dean Howells might have been. Yet, whatever Percy's hopes in dramatizing ordeal, he really presents in Binx a staged search and a staged conversion. The outcome was never in doubt.

In a piece called a self-interview, which he wrote for *Esquire* in 1977, Percy speaks almost casually of being down in Covington doing his "sexual-theological number." The interview was probably done while he was writing *Lancelot,* also published in 1977, and obviously sexual-theological. But the remark applies to all of Percy's work, beginning with *The Moviegoer,* though in that novel these themes are concealed in analyses that use Kierkegaard and the French in emphasizing despair and alienation. But for Percy man is alienated from God, not from society. Percy is primarily a Roman Catholic novelist attempting to recall the nation (not the irrevocably lost world) back to God, much as the American Puritans wished to do with more naive and sanguine hope. His main theme is man, and, along with man, love. Sex and religion are his interests in all his novels. And his interest in marriage includes a desire to prevent overindulgence in sex and the accompanying loss of compassion that treats people as objects of pleasure and substitutes flesh for God.

The criticism of Percy's work seems to derive from false hopes that he encouraged by the manner of his first novel, which appeared to create a frenzied tragic hero. Readers expected more Franco-American agonizing, whereas in fact Percy has been remarkably consistent in his now almost too frequent iteration of the moral failure of Christendom. Disappointment with his latest novel, *The Second Coming,* derives for the most part from the failure to realize that Percy's subjects were never rebellion and philosophy or epistemology but religion and moral decline. It is true that he was opposed to the Establishment, but what he sought to substitute was some earlier Establishment, or at least some imaginary age of faith. Actually, as expression of Percy's ideas, *The Second Coming* is summary and successful. It quite as neatly rounds out a career as if it had been designed for that purpose back in the fifties when Percy was trying to sort out the differences between his own romantic self and his cultural interests. In *The Second Coming,* he lays claim to the human being's right to both human and divine love, with the suggestion that experiencing both may make a man whole.

In studying these ideas, the following essays approach Percy's work straightforwardly. The biographical chapter is followed by an essay that presents the theory of art of an artist who patently wishes to teach or—perhaps more accurately—edify. A chapter on themes deals with Percy's frequent comments in the novels and elsewhere on the weak Christianity practiced in a sentimental yet faithlessly cynical age, as well as his comments on women and blacks. Thereafter, a chapter on style deals with Percy's beautiful linguistic capabilities, especially as revealed in his strikingly apt metaphors and in his imagery. An essay on each of the novels in chronological order then traces themes of sex and religion as Percy wrestles with these essential aspects of human existence.

Jac Tharpe

University of Southern Mississippi

Acknowledgments

Lewis Lawson has been consistently responsive and pleasant, and Warren French has been very patient and helpful. Joseph Weixlmann of Indiana State University prepared the Bibliography. Cheryl Saunders cheerfully read portions of the manuscript. Wallace Kay, dean of the Honors College, has often allowed me to take advantage of his kindness, and I have consistently enjoyed the support of the administration of the University of Southern Mississippi.

Abbreviations

Chronology

Chapter One
Biography, Background, and Influences
Biography

Walker Percy was born in Alabama and spent his childhood there. His father committed suicide when Walker was thirteen, and his mother was killed about two years later in an automobile accident. He and his two younger brothers were adopted by their father's cousin, William Alexander Percy, who lived in Greenville, Mississippi. Uncle Will, as they called him, was a "bachelor-poet-lawyer-planter," as Percy later said,[1] and he was father to the boys until his death in 1942. Percy says, "He certainly had a powerful influence on me. The whole idea of the Greek-Roman Stoic view, the classical view, was exemplified in him more than in any other person I ever knew."[2] He probably serves as the pattern for Aunt Emily in *The Moviegoer*. His own literary work was considerable, and he attracted a good many intellectuals to his plantation in Greenville.

Walker entered the University of North Carolina in 1934, where he majored in chemistry. He graduated in 1937 and then went to study medicine at Columbia College of Physicians and Surgeons. During this period, he had three years of Freudian analysis, an experience he may have recalled in the early part of *The Last Gentleman*. Though he received his degree and interned in pathology, he has never practiced medicine. While working as a pathologist at Bellevue in New York City, he got tuberculosis, because, according to the story, he and his colleagues failed to wear masks and gloves as they worked.[3] He spent two years at Saranac Lake in the New York Adirondacks; later, while he was teaching pathology at Columbia Medical School, a relapse sent him to another hospital, Gaylord Farms in Connecticut. During this period of convalescence he read French and Russian literature as well as Kierkegaard.

After his recovery, he and Shelby Foote, who was himself to become a Mississippi novelist, traveled to Santa Fé, an experience possibly used in *The Last Gentleman* as well as in some of the essays that mention the Grand Canyon. Percy returned and married a nurse whom he had met during a summer of work at a clinic in Greenville. They went to live for awhile in Sewanee, Tennessee, where his cousin Will owned some property, and years later some details of that area's cove and cave geography appeared in the physical setting for *The Second Coming*. In this Episcopal center, he was converted to Catholicism.

The Percys moved to New Orleans in 1947 and then, possibly because, as Binx Bolling says in *The Moviegoer*, he was tired of watching the sidewalk connoisseurs on Royal Street, they moved just across Lake Pontchartrain to the north to Covington, Louisiana, where they have lived since 1950. This area is probably the general setting for *Love in the Ruins*.

The Percys have two children, girls, one of whom was born deaf, and this condition may have inspired Percy's interest in language. He repeatedly says in some of the essays in *The Message in the Bottle* that thinking about Helen Keller's experience led him to theorize about what he calls his triadic theory of symbol and meaning, an interaction unique to human beings involving the relationship among a person, an object, and the word that names the object; thus a relationship between man and nature that language establishes and maintains.

A passage from the beginning of *The Last Gentleman* sounds autobiographical. Will has just seen Kitty in Central Park.

What distinguished him anyhow was this: he had to know everything before he could do anything. For example, he had to know what other people's infirmities were before he could get on a footing with them. . . . His life had come to such a pass that he attached significance to it. For until this moment he had lived in a state of pure possibility, not knowing what sort of a man he was or what he must do, and supposing therefore that he must be all men and do everything. But after this morning's incident his life took a turn in a particular direction. Thereafter he came to see that he was not destined to do everything but only one or two things. Lucky is the man who does not secretly believe that every possibility is open to him. (*LG*, 3–4)

Hints in the few autobiographical accounts and in the interviews suggest that the novels do provide some information about Percy. In fact, the first three novels appear to deal with avatars of the author. Binx is the puritanic sophisticate who knows what he thinks, but Will seems like "a raw youth," "a youth whose only talent was a knack for looking and listening, for tuning in and soaking up."[4] Advice to watch and wait is what Will gives to David, the innocent black in *The Last Gentleman,* and he intensifies his own apprenticeship to Sutter. This essay on "Uncle Will" mentions the death of Percy's mother, the Capehart record player, the moral stance that resembles that of Will's father in *The Last Gentleman,* the stoic philosophy of Uncle Will, and the observation: " 'Fornicating like white trash is one thing, but leave it to this age to call it the new morality.' "

Luschei, who interviewed Percy, says: "One has only to be with him for a few minutes to recognize the cant-free solidity of the man whose pilgrimage is charted in his novels. He does not see himself particularly in a literary role; writing novels is one of the things he does. Directly confronted on the question, he identifies himself as a failed physician. Pressed for positive definitions, he adds that he is a person who takes an interest in something and sees it through."[5]

In a piece for *Esquire,* Percy speaks of a portrait of himself "over the fireplace" and says,

I identify the subject of the portrait as a kind of composite of the protagonists of my novels, but most especially Lancelot. He is not too attractive a fellow and something of a nut besides. As we say in the South, he's mean as a yard dog. It is not a flattering portrait—he is not the sort of fellow you'd like to go fishing with. He is, as usual, somewhat out of it, out of the world that is framed off behind him. Where is he? It is an undisclosed place, a kind of limbo. It's a dark place—look at that background—if one believed in auras, his would be a foreboding one. It is a kind of desert, a bombed-out place, a place after the end of the world, a no-man's-land of blasted trees and barbed wire. As for him, he is neither admirable nor attractive. Rather, he is cold-eyed and sardonic. There is a gleam in his eyes, a muted and dubious satisfaction. He is looking straight at the viewer, soliciting him ironically: *"You and I know something, don't we?"*[6]

And he goes on. The facetious manner seems quite like that of the author of *The Last Gentleman* and perhaps like that of Tom More, someone who "loves his fellowman hardly at all" (*LR,* 6). Whatever may be Percy's character, he has a finely wrought ironic mind, a healthy approach to human antics through satire, and a good sense of humor.

Background

Walker Percy lived in the South until he entered medical school at Columbia in 1937. In 1944, after his recovery from tuberculosis, he returned to the South, where he has remained except for traveling. A short time was spent in Tennessee, and the rest of his life was spent in Alabama, Mississippi, and Louisiana. He maintains that the South no longer exists as the fairly well-defined region of seg-regationists, agrarians, and romantic pastoralists, and he has gone to some trouble to iterate the point.[7] Yet his several protestations help to create another new South. In *The Last Gentleman,* Will Barrett returns to a South "different from the South he had left. It was happy, victorious, Christian, rich, patriotic and Republican" (*LG,* 185). And, as Percy notes elsewhere, every Southern writer has to come to terms with the Negro question.[8] No "Northern" novelist discusses either religion or blacks as much as Percy does. Few Southerners discuss blacks and religion as much as Percy does, for that matter, though of course his moral stance requires him to deal with precisely those two important concerns.

Percy's views on equality for the Negro are those of a "Southern moderate," his own phrase, presented in essays written during the major attempts at integration back in the sixties. In the seventies, the matter is less important: Lance, who was for a time a civil rights lawyer, has by time of publication in 1977 begun handling title searches for ordinary exchanges of property. But while Percy has no illusions about Southern arguments for the value of paternalism, he also suspects Northern politicians of counting the Negro vote when talking of equality. Finally, Percy has no illusions about the Negro's capacity to achieve anything more in the way of humanity to man than his white brethren have achieved, while he recognizes the Negro's "right" to alienation.[9]

Presumably with his conversion to Roman Catholicism, a growing awareness of personal alienation as well as a growing emotion about the failure of the Christian church led Percy to something resembling a reassessment of Christian orthodoxy and a moral code. Awareness of the widespread inhuman treatment of blacks by whites claiming to be Christian must have contributed to his emotions. Then, as America became a sexual wasteland, he developed an idea resembling that of Will's father in *The Last Gentleman*, a gentleman who killed himself in part because the world had arrived at the low point where the sexual immorality of the best people resembled that of the trash. The distinction Aunt Emily makes among classes in *The Moviegoer* has vanished. Christian doctrine has, as Percy tells one interviewer, always considered man alienated: "alienation, after all, is nothing more or less than a very ancient, orthodox Christian doctrine. Man is alienated by the nature of his being here."[10] Thus, the idea that absorbs Percy was old long before the existentialists began talking about it and before they influenced him in choosing it for writing novels.

Percy's first publications were linguistic and philosophical essays (published in 1975 as *The Message in the Bottle*) dealing generally with anthropology in the broad sense of man's being and purpose, especially as exemplified in the mystery of language and symbol. While Percy often treated these ideas separately, they are actually alternative approaches to the idea of God's relationship to man.

Percy's interest in writing appears at least as early as 1935, when he was at North Carolina in school. He wrote a little for *Carolina Magazine*, and one essay showed some knowledge of the movies.[11] Thereafter, he seems to have worked along at writing while his friend Shelby Foote was publishing.[12] But Percy published nothing until 1954, when "Symbol as Need" appeared in response to Suzanne Langer's *Feeling and Form*. Other philological and epistemological essays quickly followed during the decade. Then, in 1961, he published *The Moviegoer*, for which he received the National Book Award. As he continued to publish occasional essays, he wrote the other five novels, the last of which appeared in 1980. Meanwhile, he became a kind of spokesman for the South, even as he claimed it no longer existed separately as a cultural entity.

Influences

"I guess," Percy says, "my main debt to Kierkegaard is the use of his tremendous philosophical and theological insight as a basis to build on."[13] But, he adds, "I was always put off by Kierkegaard's talk about inwardness, subjectivity, and the absurd, the leap into the absurd."[14] These elements of the romanticism of the early nine-teenth century, which may account for much of Kierkegaard's re-belliousness and emphasis on the value of individual experience, have little appeal to the Catholic novelist who wishes to deal with men in real situations, the basic premise of a Percy novel (see chapter 2). Whatever the extent of Kierkegaard's influence,[15] Percy no doubt found appeal in Kierkegaard's attack on Hegel's attempt to ration-alize the universe and in Kierkegaard's emphasis on the church's assurance of salvation acquired through practice of uniform ritual and sacrament. This and other aspects of the romantic attack on Christendom, along with that of Emerson and the English lyric poets, ought to have appealed to Percy's idea of the individual's responsibility for his life and salvation. Percy so much encourages in the major early interviews (see Bibliography) Kierkegaardian interpretations of his work as to limit and distort his own themes. And a long essay in Luschei's work emphasizes this influence.

Percy has also mentioned in "From Facts to Fiction" (as noted above) the influence of the French existentialists, whom he read during his recuperation from tuberculosis. Sartre's *Nausea* and *The Age of Reason* seem to be obvious influences in their concern with the malaise of the nineteenth and twentieth centuries as well as their use of real situations. Sartre's word *nausea* is one name for the malaise and its association with everydayness and boredom. Both Camus and Sartre were concerned with the authentic life—courage at living as displayed in the individual's choice among alternatives without, ironically, the abstract assurance of precisely such insti-tutions as the church. Percy of course encourages choice between church and the various utopias and other "angelistic" enterprises that men have developed. Aside from this general existentialist view shared with Sartre and Camus, specifically in *The Moviegoer* the vagaries of the love affair between Binx and Kate may be determined by the liaison in *The Age of Reason,* and Camus's *The Stranger* appears in the alienation as well as the "conversion" of Percy's moviegoer. *The Fall* probably accounts for the strident tone of *Lancelot.* In discussing that novel, Percy says: "I owe a debt to Camus. In his novel, 'The Fall,' one man talked to another man, and that's the way it goes in mine. It's an interesting form and a difficult one, something like a dramatic morality play."[16] Heidegger and Ortega y Gassett are among several figures of the twentieth century men-tioned here and there in Percy's essays; so are Marcel and Merleau-

Ponty. The ambiguity of Binx's commitment and "conversion" at the end of *The Moviegoer* may derive specifically from Evelyn Waugh's *Brideshead Revisited,* at the end of which the unbeliever prays in a chapel. The bibliography to *The Message in the Bottle* shows a wide reading knowledge. In addition, Wittgenstein, himself influenced by Kierkegaard, may have exerted an influence on Percy's *Lancelot,* where the curious unspeakability of love is at issue.

Dostoevski's intense characters as well as their passionate concern with Christianity and associated concepts of guilt, sin, crime, and love must have been attractive. *The Moviegoer,* written mostly from Mrs. Schexnaydre's basement, sometimes resembles the contradictory approach revealed in the monologue of the underground man. Percy says the last scene of that novel uses the last scene with Alyosha and the children from *The Brothers Karamazov.*[17] Some of Sutter's traits, in *The Last Gentleman,* may derive from both the intellectual Ivan and the sensualist Dimitri in *The Brothers Karamazov,* as well as from the bedeviled Stavrogin in *The Possessed.* Dimitri's claim to love woman resembles the inclination in Percy's characters. Percy refers in the essays to *War and Peace,* traces of which may appear throughout his first three novels.

Love in the Ruins was intended as, among other things, a synthesis of important Western documents. The first few lines paraphrase the beginning of *The Divine Comedy.* Both Faust and Don Juan legends appear in the narrative: one an individual damned because of pride, the other because of love. Sir Thomas More is cited here and there in that novel, and other utopians are suggested by association with the subject matter. Maybe something of Gargantua is there in Tom's zest for life and something of *The Praise of Folly* in his foolishness. Actually, Tom's reference to Sir Thomas More's humor even at the time of his death recalls the holy fool in the Christian tradition as well as the idea of praising folly.[18]

Lancelot recalls not only numerous Arthurian romances, including those dealing with the quest for the grail, but also Tolstoi's *Kreuzer Sonata,* in which a jealous husband kills his wife and which is also largely a monologue.

American figures appear to be in Percy's background too. His consistent symbolic use of white recalls Poe's narrative of A. Gordon Pym and Melville's attachment to the shadelessness of white in both *White Jacket* and *Moby Dick.* The unpardonable sin of Hawthorne is recalled in Lancelot's quest, and "My Kinsman, Major Molineux" promotes a bemused youth whom the narrator ironically labels shrewd, somewhat like Will Barrett. And Hawthorne invented the American theological novel.

Emerson and Whitman as theorists of American culture and its relationship to the artist and his art have anticipated Percy's work whether or not they influenced Percy. Emerson discussed a concept of self-reliance in ethics and religious matters, and in his essay on the subject says, "Man is timid and apologetic; he is no longer upright; he dares not say 'I think,' 'I am,' but quotes some saint or sage. He is ashamed before the blade of grass or the blowing rose." Emerson, who opposed even monotheism as well as the Trinity, went farther than Percy; and his concept of nature was of the unity of being, though he went beyond Percy's Aquinean concern with a natural unity of body and soul. Emerson might have said man "spends his life as though he were not the center of the supreme mystery but rather diverting himself"[19] or (almost) "Either we have outgrown monotheism, and good riddance; or modern man is estranged from being, from his own being, from the being of other creatures in the world, from transcendent being. He has lost something, what he does not know; he knows only that he is sick unto death with the loss of it."[20] Emerson, too, was interested in the original uses of language and the original meanings of words, and his theorizing about the nature of poetry anticipates Whitman's concept of the poet as priest, which could be adapted to Percy's theory of art.

Further, in Percy's own South are the fugitives and the agrarians,[21] among them Warren, Ransom, and Tate, Ransom especially saying no in thunder, as Percy does. *God Without Thunder* lashes out at science and criticizes industrialization and technology. *The World's Body* calls for an old individualism. A pastoral idealistic old order, possibly not quite Augustinian but sounding Christian, was one of the main ideals of the group. Percy often sounds as if his Roman Catholicism were coming from the impulse that gave impetus to Southern pastoralism and other conservative views of anthropology.

Chapter Two
Theory of Art

Percy's theory of art assumes that the artist will participate in society rather than withdraw from it to the palace of art or the ivory tower. Art contributes to anthropology, as Percy uses the concept, to refer to the study of man in the broadest sense, to his existence, predicament, and purpose. He says, "The function of writers and novelists and poets is probably the highest in the culture, because their job is to make people understand themselves."[1] (While he talks occasionally of other forms of art, he generally refers to the novel.) His theories about art are framed within the lines of three of his main interests: his studies of language as uniquely defining man and separating him from the rest of creation; his quarrel with a science that appears to know all but which tells man nothing about his uniqueness; and especially his devotion to Roman Catholicism, which deals with the mystery that man is.

On this third point, Percy says his work as a novelist is automatically shaped by his religion:

as a writer you have a certain view of man, a certain view of the way it is, and even if you don't recognize it or even if you disavow such a view, you can't escape that view or lack of view. . . . I think my writings reflect a certain basic orientation toward, although they're not really controlled by, Catholic dogma. . . . So, to me, the Catholic view of man as pilgrim, in transit, in journey, is very compatible with the vocation of a novelist because a novelist is writing about man in transit, man as pilgrim. I think it would be a disadvantage, for example, to be a Freudian and a novelist.[2]

Helping people to understand themselves shapes his view—not his method: "I think I am conscious of the danger of the novelist trying to draw a moral," he says.[3] For "A novelist least of all has the authority to edify anyone or tell them good news, to pronounce

Christ King."[4] This view appears in Binx's disclaimer at the end of *The Moviegoer* as to the purpose of his narrative (*M*, 237). Yet, Percy says, "I've always been a polemicist and a moralist."[5] And he often shows moral indignation. He has repeatedly said in interviews that he feels "a good deal of energy in my writing comes from a passion or strong feeling on something. . . . And I think it works both ways. A man has to have some sort of passion, either a dislike for something—love or malice—to have enough energy to write about it."[6] He tells another interviewer that the "main motivation, the wellspring of my writing . . . , is usually antagonism, disagreeing with somebody and wanting to get it right."[7] His novels are generally dramatized on the dialectic of antagonism, the expression of opposing points of view.

In 1977, about the time he would have been writing *Lancelot* with its diatribes, he wrote an essay called "The State of the Novel," in which he says, "The novelist or poet may in his own perverse way be a modern version of the Old-Testament prophet who . . . finds himself stuck with the unpleasant assignment of pointing out to his fellow citizens that something is wrong, that they are on the wrong track."[8]

A major function of the artist is, then, communication:

in league with the individual, with his need to have himself confirmed in his predicament. It is the artist who at his best reverses the alienating process by the very act of seeing it clearly for what it is and naming it, and who in this same act establishes a kind of community. It is a paradoxical community whose members are both alone yet not alone, who strive to become themselves and discover that there are others who, however tentatively, have undertaken the same quest.[9]

Implicit in such theorizing is of course the idea of a communion of saints, orthodox religious doctrine, and, perhaps, the concept of a purge of impurities. But what Percy seems to consider important he elaborates randomly. This communication, basically linguistic theory, he diagrams as a triad analogous to the triad used in his theory of language. In the linguistic theory of meaning, the object has a name given by a namer for communication with a hearer. This is the process of symbolization, on which communication is based. Similarly, the novel is the means of communication between artist and reader. By this means, the knowledge is transmitted by the

artist and learned by the reader. (By this means, too, both the artist
who can talk about it and the reader who can read about it may
attenuate the despair of alienation, according to Percy's claims.)
Herein specifically is art used for social, even religious, purposes,
to the extent that Percy deals with personal salvation within the
framework of Christianity, as he appears ultimately to do. Only the
novelist can adequately deal with alienation. Ultimately art for Percy
is a means for an intersubjective relationship (his term) that allows
people to become what he calls co-celebrants of being.[10] In theological terms, salvation is the message and the reward.

Art Teaches

Percy also makes for art the traditional claim that it teaches quite
as distinctly as science does:

> My theory is that the purpose of art is to transmit universal truths of a
> sort, but of a particular sort, that in art, whether it's poetry, fiction or
> painting, you are telling the reader or the listener or the viewer something
> he already knows but which he doesn't quite know that he knows, so that
> in the action of communication he experiences a recognition, a feeling
> that he has been there before, a shock of recognition. And so, what the
> artist does, or tries to do, is simply to validate the human experience and
> to tell people the deep human truths which they already unconsciously
> know.[11]

This combination of romantic theory and Platonic epistemology
leads also to the claim "that serious novel writing, that serious art,
is just as important, and just as cognitive; it concerns areas of
knowing, of discovering and knowing, just as much as any science. . . . I think that the serious novelist is quite as much concerned with discovering reality as the serious physicist."[12] Elsewhere
he says, science "can say nothing about what a man is or what he
must do. And then the question is, how do you deal with man?
And if you are an anthropologist in the larger sense, interested in
man, how do you study him? And it seemed to me that the novel
itself was a perfectly valid way to deal with man's behavior."[13]

The novel studies human behavior and presents conclusions. Thus,
one does not write "enigmas and acrostics," nor does the artist "have
a thesis and then illustrate it. What you do is put a man in a certain
situation and see what happens. . . . and I was interested in phe-

nomenology, which is very strongly existentialist: the idea of describing accurately how a man feels in a given situation. And that's certainly novelistic."[14]

In a symposium held in 1975, Percy elucidates his theory that art is cognitive.

> When I speak of recognition and verification and cognition in fiction, I'm thinking, say of passages in certain novels which have given me great pleasure. For example, the passage in James Agee at the beginning of the prologue to *A Death in the Family* in which he describes the quality of life on a summer afternoon in Knoxville and the quality of the consciousness of the boy who's with his father and living and seeing the life and smelling the smells of Knoxville. What I experience is a recognition and a formulation, a concept, if you like, of something which I have been vaguely aware of but which had not been formulated by me by such exquisite symbols and sentences. I cannot describe this transaction in any other way than a cognition, a reception of a formulation from a writer to a reader.

He does not elaborate the point especially well; rather on this same occasion, he repeats: "I find myself always in sympathy with the esthetic, first of Suzanne Langer and people as different as Maritain and going back originally to Thomas Aquinas, who said in different ways, that art is a form of knowing. It's a kind of knowledge which is quite different from discursive knowledge and mathematical knowledge." Furthermore, he says, "It's hard for me to imagine any novelist not being motivated by some desire to approach some kind of truth or what he thinks to be the truth."[15]

While Percy reiterates his claim that art tells the truth and contributes to knowledge, he feels that storytelling has less importance now than it had in the nineteenth century, when the novel dealt with and emerged from an "intact society, . . . where people understood who they were and what they were doing," a situation that allowed plot and characterization. Now, though, "to the degree that a novel reflects life, I think that the modern novel has become much more fragmented, without a strong and conventional plot and all that."[16] Thus, he says, "I'm not interested in storytelling as such. I'm interested in it for what it tells me of what people do, how they behave, and why."[17]

But while the novel may deal with issues that are or should be of current interest, it must not deal with abstractions. "A novelist should be concerned with what is the case in the world, the facts, the richness, the intricacy and the variety of the way things are."[18] When he wrote *The Moviegoer,* he says, he decided to deal "with a *man* who finds himself in a *world,* a very concrete man who is located in a very concrete place and time. Such a man might be represented as *coming to himself* in somewhat the same sense as Robinson Crusoe came to himself on his island after his shipwreck, with the same wonder and curiosity."[19] When an interviewer says he feels Percy's first two novels deal with "an idea or theme, rather than with a character," Percy replies, "I would rather say they start with a situation." In *The Moviegoer,* he goes on to say, he was "concerned with a certain quality of consciousness put down in a certain place and then seeing what kind of reaction takes place between a character and his environment and the people he meets."[20] Such a procedure apparently allows a good deal of satire and ironic comment from that particular observer. But one emphasis here is upon what people do: "the novel has to do with *action,* with an encounter between two people."[21] Percy speaks literally of emphasizing what people do, not what individuals do, for he does not characterize brilliantly, despite his interest in the psychological and the grotesque. When he says "My characters are all fairly recognizable,"[22] he in effect says they are types. His interest is in what the activity is and often in whether it is moral or immoral.

Language and Art

Language itself is the source of some aspect of the knowledge derived from art. Like many others, Percy deplores the abuse of language. In an interview, he identifies several worn-out theological concepts: "Particularly religious words: baptism, sin, God."[23] But he proposes to freshen language with new metaphors, thus teaching both writer and reader. "Metaphors," he says, "are very strange because when you put two things together it's a way of discovering meanings which haven't been discovered before. It's a very strange thing because you discover meanings which you know, and the reader knows, but neither one of you knew that you knew until you see it discovered by a new metaphor."[24] While Percy devises many metaphors that illustrate his theory of practice without usually appearing contrived, his real talent in writing lies in his concrete use of language to describe, particularly, physical nature. He is often rich in the most perceptive and original fashion.

In "Metaphor as Mistake," he seems to refer to metaphor that appears as the result of a mistake, misunderstanding, ignorance, or some unusual intuition. Through metaphor, "whether it's deliberate or done by mistake," he says, "I think that's the way language renews itself."[25] He cites as example a black in Alabama calling the blue darter hawk a blue dollar hawk. Another example appears in *Lancelot*, when a black guide to the Southern mansion refers to bibelots as bilbos. Renewal by mistake comments wryly on the possibility of precision in language. But what Percy is really concerned with in these comments may be the metaphysical relationship between language and being, somewhat as Heidegger discussed the matter.[26] A reviewer of *The Message in the Bottle*, in which Percy expresses his views on language, says, "Accidental metaphor points to the magic of the naming process by which man can formalize the vivid emotional experience of an object and thus assert his right to see and to know it."[27] Insights into this theory of metaphor may be offered by two other reviewers.

For Percy finds meaning in incongruity. He suggests in fact that we all do. And that is the essence of "How Queer Man Is."
    Percy feels that it is the essence of human nature to see one thing through another. Thus we need the name to know the thing and the thing to know the name. We find particular pleasure when totally disparate and unexpected words and things are yoked together. That is why metaphor is "wrongest when it is most beautiful."[28]

Finally,

Hence mistakes and misunderstandings are seen as exemplary because they eliminate the straightforwardly descriptive or functional use of names and dramatize instead their separate but equal ontological status. Denotation is thus a "coupling" of two different and distinct elements, and it is only by means of this coupling, Percy says, that we can begin to comprehend the world. "It is *only* if you say what the object *is* that you can know anything about it at all." By speaking of things you can understand them.[29]

Whatever the theory, one of the distinctions of Percy's writing is numerous metaphors, rarely from mistake, rather from deliberation and originality.

Southern Literature

Whatever his Southern heritage, from Flannery O'Connor, Faulkner, or the agrarians, Percy has consistently maintained as a part of his theorizing about the novel that a distinctive Southern literature is no longer tenable as a concept. He says in a recent article,

to me as a writer, it appears that what needs, not so much defending as understanding, reconciling, rejoicing in, ridiculing, cracking jokes about, healing, affirming, is not the Southern experience but the American experience. And since every writer must write of his own experience—or else not write at all—the Southern writer necessarily writes of the South, but he writes of it in terms which are immediately translatable to the American experience and, if he is good enough, to the human experience.[30]

"I think," he said some years earlier, "that the day of regional Southern writing is all gone," though, he adds, "If I were in Colorado or New York, I'd be writing something different." Furthermore, "I think what we're stuck with in the South and what's of value are two things: one is religion and the other is the Negro."[31]

But Percy claims that these matters of religion and Negroes are moral failures of the nation, not mainly the South. He claims that he is one of those among several artists who find that

something has gone badly wrong with Americans and American life, indeed modern life, that people generally suffer a deep dislocation in their lives which has nothing to do with poverty and ignorance and discrimination. Indeed it is the very people who have escaped Tobacco Road and moved to the exurbs who have fallen victim to this malaise. What increasingly engages the Southern novelist as much as his Connecticut counterpart are no longer the Snopeses or Popeyes or O'Connor's crackers or Wright's black underclass but their successful grandchildren who are going nuts in Atlanta condominiums.[32]

The fact is that Percy himself is the only major writer in America who is writing about religion at all and the only one who is writing about blacks in the South. Other writers have written about blacks, though not the white artists, and James Baldwin has written about the blacks in the South, but Percy is unique in writing about precisely the two subjects, religion and blacks, most distinctly associated with Southern literature and the South.

Percy does not have the Southern enclave associated with Faulkner or the small townishness of Eudora Welty or the peculiar grotesqueries of Flannery O'Connor, Carson McCullers, or Poe. But in writing about what he knows, he uses some aspect of the South for all of his settings, though he avoids anything that would particularly suggest local color.

Truth and Beauty

It is, or course, evident that Percy has a message, no matter how well it is concealed in his art and no matter how well he avoids what Binx calls "the edifying." But finally, as if nonchalantly, he mentions the traditional concerns of the artist: "The artist, as Joyce said a while back, has to be a cunning, guileful fellow who uses every trick in the bag for his own good ends, these ends being presumably and among other things the trapping of the reader into revelations of truth, beauty and suchlike."[33] This sounds a little like a utilitarian theory of didacticism and edification, despite the disclaimers quoted above. Beauty is in the service of truth, which may be right. Percy's particular good end is the "truth" he mentions above in the symposium transcript, and it is the truth of a Christian moralist. On this subject, John Gardner, the American novelist, made some remarks when reviewing *Lancelot* in 1977, after Percy had been writing novels for fifteen years. "Fiction, at its best," Gardner says, "is a means of discovery, a philosophical method. By that standard, Walker Percy is not a very good novelist: in fact 'Lancelot,' for all its dramatic and philosophical intensity, is bad art, and what's worse, typical bad art. . . . it fools around with philosophy . . . for fashionable groans. Art, it seems to me, should be a little less pompous, a lot more serious. It should stop sniveling and go for answers or else shut up."[34] A good many readers might agree with Gardner on all points. *Lancelot* does play with philosophy, and it is boring when it plays. Besides, the question is whether the theological novel, specifically the Christian theological novel, has any value—whether Christian theology has any significance any more. Does Percy have anything to say when he talks, or does he just often talk pretty, like a politician or a preacher or a medicine man? Speaking of medicine men, Percy, as noted above, thinks the artist is one. And perhaps he ought to have the last word if only to repeat himself: "Depicting the commonplace," he says in a self-interview, "allows the reader to penetrate the commonplace."

If such a person, a person like me feeling lapsed at four o'clock in the afternoon, should begin reading a novel about a person feeling lapsed at four o'clock in the afternoon, a strange thing happens. Things increase in value. Possibilities open. This may be the main function of art in this peculiar age: to reverse the devaluation. What the artist or writer does is not depict a beautiful tree—this only depresses you more than ever—no, he depicts the commonplaceness of an everyday tree. Depicting the commonplace allows the reader to penetrate the commonplace. The only other way the husk of the commonplace can be penetrated is through the occurrence of natural disasters or the imminence of one's own death. These measures are not readily available on ordinary afternoons.[35]

Chapter Three
Christendom

Christianity

The church is always in the background of Walker Percy's novels. *The Moviegoer*, his first novel, only intimates its influence in the plan of the novels, but it remains a force throughout, reaching a climax of influence in *Love in the Ruins*, the third novel. Being Christian means for Percy an interest in reform and in morality, particularly sexual morality, and an active reaffirmation of faith in the basic doctrines of Roman Catholicism. For Percy, as for the Roman church, marriage is still a sacrament. Though Percy does not evangelize, each novel ends with some form of epiphany. In the tradition of the prophets and the moralists, he threatens that reform is urgent before the time is too late in "these dread latter days" of *Love in the Ruins*, and he may even at times suggest that the second coming is at hand. He does not argue for asceticism; rather, he displays a high regard for nature, in which man was made to live and enjoy the world.

Despite some ambiguity used to avoid didacticism, each novel asserts a creed. Binx Bolling in *The Moviegoer* moves to what Percy, using Kierkegaard's term, calls the religious stage. In *The Last Gentleman*, Will Barrett, according to Percy, begins his search in the religious stage even if he fails to see the epiphany. (Both observations are cited below.) *Love in the Ruins*, subtitled *The Adventures of a Bad Catholic Near the End of the World*, narrates, among numerous other things, the main character's gradual return to the church. At the end of *Lancelot*, the long-silent figure called Percival has renewed his vows and decided to become an anonymous man of God in a small church in Alabama. At the end of *The Second Coming*, an anatomy of belief, Will Barrett, with a second chance, chooses to hope—after travail with unbelief in the worthless. Earlier, among the essays, Percy was fairly explicit about his religious interests, in, for example, "Notes for a Novel about the End of the World." But "The Message in the Bottle," intended as a "discussion of a piece of news in an information system, how to classify it as a serious statement,"[1] ends with a beautiful statement of hope: "And what if the news the newsbearer bears is the very news the castaway had been waiting for, news of where he came from and who he is, and what he must do, and what if the newsbearer brought with him the means by which the castaway may do what he must do? Well then, the castaway will, by the grace of God, believe him" (*MB*, 149).

Attack

Percy's work is also an attack on Christendom. Like Kierkegaard, from whom the specific idea and the expression are taken, Percy distinguishes between Christendom and Christianity. Christianity is the uncluttered central body of Christian doctrine, with its concept of God's grace and individual salvation through a personal savior. Christianity is a way of living and a concept of eternal life. Christendom is the geographical area, the realm of Christianity, as opposed to that of Islam or Buddhism, which has nourished the fantastic institution that has formed in association with Christianity, without regard for Christian doctrines. Christendom is characterized especially by its great moral failure. It has consistently either compromised with political tyranny or been responsible for political tyranny. Christendom is the area in which European politics rarely allowed Christian ideals to influence decisions and in which nowadays talk of Christianity is useless. Christendom is characterized by the "enlightened" inclination to explain and forgive all bad conduct as beyond the power of human responsibility. For Percy, Sweden is the ultimate example of what Christendom has done: established in the so-called Christian world a welfare state that cares for a man from cradle to grave.

Christendom is replete with worn religious symbols, particularly church edifices. In *The Second Coming,* on his way to play golf, Will Barrett "drove through town on Church Street. . . . He passed . . . the Christian Church, Church of Christ, Church of God, Church of God in Christ, Church of Christ in God, Assembly of God, Bethel Baptist Church, Independent Presbyterian Church, United Methodist Church, and Immaculate Heart of Mary Roman

Catholic Church." The list is long because "He lives in the most Christian nation in the world, the U. S. A., in the most Christian part of that nation, the South, in the most Christian state in the South, North Carolina, in the most Christian town in North Carolina" (SC, 13). In this nation, according to the statistics of Binx Bolling the businessman, ninety-eight percent believe in God. This condition of a replete and plenary Christendom with a faint Christian practice is Percy's topic: The American Christian novelist's "dilemma is that though he professes a belief which he holds saves himself and the world and nourishes his art besides . . . Christendom seems in some sense to have failed" (MB, 116).

While Percy does not attack Christendom as the romantics, Kierkegaard, and Emerson do (Emerson wishing even to reform doctrine), he is acutely aware of its shortcomings.

There is besides the devaluation of its vocabulary the egregious moral failure of Christendom . . . in the sector of everyday morality, which has acutely concerned Americans since the Puritans. Americans take pride in doing right. It is not chauvinistic to suppose that perhaps they have done righter than any other great power in history. But in the one place, the place which hurts the most and where charity was most needed, they have not done right. White Americans have sinned against the Negro from the beginning and continue to do so, initially with cruelty and presently with an indifference which may be even more destructive. (MB, 117)

In the United States, obvious indications of Christendom's moral failure are sexual unrestraint and compromise with cheap fundamentalism, mistreatment of blacks, and the inclination to stomach any combination of abstractions on the theory that a man has a right to his beliefs. Compromise with fundamentalism takes the form of drawing the sweet Jesus into everyday life with such ideas as Jesus Christ the greatest pro of them all (Love in the Ruins), the invisible golfer at the country club in Paradise Estates.

Percy's attack on Christendom is through analysis of these failures. The Moviegoer juxtaposes stoicism, a humanist creed as idealized in the Old South, and the worship of divinity as Roman Catholicism. Aunt Emily is eloquent about the virtues that stoicism supports, and the Roman Catholicism as Binx's family practices it is the simple alternative. In that novel, if Binx explicitly chooses neither way, he apparently chooses to be a sovereign wayfarer and attempts to make his "little contribution."

In *The Last Gentleman,* the dialogue is between Sutter, the atheist pornographer, and Val, the representative of Christendom; or between sex and religion, immanence and transcendence. The conflict between body and spirit that accounts for so much of the history, philosophy, and social science of Western man intensifies this dialectic.

The main theme of *Love in the Ruins* is precisely love, not utopia and not sane politics or an ideal polity. For Percy, utopias are only logical not religious. Christianity is the ideal for man. The conflict is between love of woman and love of God—sex and religion, human love and divine, human desire and divine desire.

Lancelot returns to the dialogue between alternatives in Christendom, the gentleman's code and the Christian code. The novel shows a multitude of failures.

Finally, in *The Second Coming,* Percy conjoins loves. Will rejects the whole world to save his own soul. And he seeks to build a utopia wherein man lives through God's grace, a natural state in which plants flourish and people function while they live out their days on God's green earth.

The superiority of Christianity is emphasized by a consideration of its opposite. A major aspect of Christendom is scientific humanism, the urge to establish utopias, an urge that has weakened Christianity by advancing theories of behaviorism that reduce men to creatures operating by instinct rather than freedom of choice. Denizens of this land of the good life prate of individuality when all men are anonymous. And ideals rather than practice "make" all men good as well as equal. Humanism excuses their faults and ascribes their failures to any cause except sovereign human responsibility.

Percy lets one of his humanists condemn this point of view. Aunt Emily, the old stoic, presents an ancient ideal. Her people are better, she says, because "We do not prize mediocrity for mediocrity's sake. . . . we hear a great many flattering things nowadays about your great common man. . . . he is perfectly content so to be called, because that is exactly what he is: the common man and when I say common I mean common as hell. ·. . . Ours is the only civilization in history which has enshrined mediocrity as its national ideal" (*M,* 223). Humanism can make all these entities somehow "equal" but does not give them a goal, purpose, or reason for being.

Science can make life less unpleasant but can say nothing about living. Scientific humanists of every kind fill the pages of *Love in the Ruins* and the wasteland it depicts. Among them is a biologist who has no idea how to get on with the simple business of reproduction. He even asks for an artificial sexual organ because his own natural organ will not perform. In addition to providing for the physical environment, science has offered psychoanalysis for the mentally unsettled, who are thereby encouraged to find the correct behavior for the group. A man cannot even be sick in his own way.

Negro

"Every Southern writer," Percy says, "must come to some kind of terms with the Negro. He can no more avoid it than a Negro writer can avoid writing about the white man."[2] And, he says, "a writer, with his peculiar position of being a communicator, . . . can do a great deal of good, can have a great deal of influence without compromising . . . creative endeavors. My own feeling is: I don't mind saying or writing what I think on the social issues or the race issue in the South."[3] He says he is "completely convinced of the rightness of the Negro struggle for civil rights."[4]

Percy began writing about the time the civil rights movement became important, and his novels contain blacks in significant roles and dwell on the question of racial relations. *The Moviegoer* is but slightly concerned with blacks, who appear mostly as realistic aspects of the New Orleans setting. Three figures are outstanding in the list of characters. There is Mercer, the butler and factotum in Aunt Emily's ménage, who cheats her and reads Rosicrucian literature. A second figure is the chimney sweep who appears near the end of the narrative and serves as an example for Aunt Emily's serene tirade about the evils of democracy untempered by ideals. Mercer's actions might be such as to elicit a generalization Percy makes: "In fact, if you have known many middle-class Negroes, nobody in the world is more middle-class or conventional than the middle-class Negro."[5] A third, perhaps better, example is the black who ambiguously takes communion on Ash Wednesday, near the end of *The Moviegoer*. But the fact that the black "cleaves to the more fatuous of white middle-class values"[6] does not condemn him any more than Aunt Emily does.

The Last Gentleman seriously considers civil rights, the subject that serves Percy's anger or malice, as he calls it, and provides him with the emotion that leads him to write. A long subplot running nearly throughout the novel presents a series of episodes dealing with blacks and the struggle for civil rights. Here too Percy analyzes the situation the Negro faces in his attempt to find himself.

The photographer disguised as a black, who is on his way to find evidence of segregation in Mississippi, is too obviously fatuous to take seriously, no matter what he ignores in New Jersey to search for in Mississippi. Percy begins here a balanced account of the matter, showing the hypocrisy and ignorance of the so-called Northern liberal.

Among the blacks mentioned are four who exemplify the difficulties of the Negro in the South. Possibly the most serious example of inhumanity is Sutter's second case: "Moderately obese young colored female, circa 13 . . . Cops report subject discovered in basement toilet of Emmanuel Baptist Church following explosion. Church tower fell on her" (*LG,* 307). This awesome failure of Christian practice is only one of the reasons that Sutter condemns Christendom.

Another incident deals with the youthful and ungainly David, the Vaughts' houseboy, who, despite his heavy accent, dreams of being a radio announcer. Will's speech to him may be a repetition of one he has heard from his father: "They're going to violate you and it's going to ruin us all, you, them, us. . . . It's God's terrible vengeance upon us . . . to leave you here among us with this fearful vulnerability to invite violation and to be violated . . ." (*LG,* 198). Possibly the Faulknerian style is unavoidable with the subject.

Most of the subplot of *The Last Gentleman* shows the oversimplified approach of most people North and South to a complex question. The photographer and his friends are among the "outside agitators" that Southerners often, sometimes rightly, blamed for racial unrest, and their antics are ridiculous to both whites and blacks. Amid all the activity is, however, a scene that dramatizes all the great wrong in Southern treatment of blacks. When Forney and his companions finally attract the addled Will's attention, on the street in Ithaca, they all congregate in the saloon operated by Sweet Evening Breeze, an effeminate black who had known Will through the years. The police are threatening, and Breeze is jittery. Will is trying to aid in the escape of the agitators, among them a white female companion to a white actor. But the black playwright is there, along with the "black" Forney. The officers burst in:

The doorway was first flooded by sunlight, then darkened by uniforms. . . .
"Where's the poontang?" asked Beans Ross, a strong, tall, fat man with a handsome tanned face and green-tinted sunglasses. . . . Beans took from his pocket a small blackjack as soft and worn as skin. . . .
"All right, Breeze," said Beans in a routine voice, not looking at him. Sweet Evening Breeze, knowing what was expected of him, doffed his stocking and presented the crown of his head. Hardly watching but with a quick outward flick of his wrist, Beans hit Breeze on the forehead with the blackjack. Breeze fell down. (*LG*, 324).

This is genuinely appalling. Though Will floors Beans shortly thereafter, no punishment could fit the crime and no treatment better show, with so few words in a space so small, the disregard for life this one man shows another.

But the incident that best analyzes the case occurs when Will meets a young man his own age on the street in Ithaca, Will himself having returned home to discover he has no home: "The engineer looked at the other as the half second wore on. You may be in a fix and I know that but what you don't know and won't believe and must find out for yourself is that I'm in a fix too and you got to get where I am before you even know what I'm talking about and I know that and that's why there is nothing to say now. Meanwhile I wish you well" (*LG*, 333). These are the words of a man who knows loss. What Will cannot say, both because he cannot be cruel and because the black would not believe him serious, is that blacks must reach the economic level the whites have attained, and then suffer the alienation the whites endure, to discover that nobody has any home.

Love in the Ruins deals explicitly with racial matters, both because the novel was written during the sixties and because Percy is dramatizing in this novel of the "dread latter days" the two moral failures of Christendom—sex and segregation. As Tom describes Paradise Estates, he shows how Northerners have easily picked up Southern ways: "Little black jockeys fish from mirrors in their front yards. Life-size mammy-dolls preside over their patios" (*LR*, 17). Racial distinction easily emerges, and subjugation is symbolized in the insensitive cute. Thus is life in Paradise Estates. Monsignor Schleifkopf (Knothead) of the American Catholic Church based in Cicero, Illinois, says on Property Rights Sunday, "a major feast day" (*LR*, 181), " 'Our Lord himself, remember, was not a social reformer, said nothing about freeing the slaves, nor are we obliged to' " (*LR*, 182).

In a special short section ending the tape recorded account of July Fourth, Tom asks, "was it the nigger business," from the beginning that led to failure of the only Christian nation, the United States? God led the Christians to a new Eden, where he required them to "pass one little test." They had, he said, "already passed the big one"—in accepting the idea that God entered history with the incarnation of divinity among the Jews. "One little test: here's a helpless man in Africa, all you have to do is not violate him" (*LR*, 57).

According to Uru, Christendom has been even more ironic in its treatment of blacks. It "enslaved" them to its religious creed, training them not only to keep the peace but also to suffer injury to innocence. The whites used Christianity not to make themselves Christian but to keep the enslaved savages tame and docile in their degradation.

But Percy does not pronounce on the matter. One view is that "The test was too much! . . . Yet even so we almost passed." Nobody ever asked anything of Russians, the speaker says, and "Who ever imagined the Chinese were blessed by God and asked to save the world?" (*LR*, 57).

Later, Tom argues with Uru, the militant black with the doctorate, who is attempting to direct the revolution. Uru has determined plans for a new society and says to Tom: " 'Only you don't think we can do it, do you?' " Tom says, " 'Look at Liberia. You've had Haiti even longer' " (*LR*, 300). Tom finally tells Uru that the blacks not only failed in Liberia and the Dominican Republic. He also says he understands what they do not—that they must get where they think we are and then see and know our malaise.

Lancelot has little to do with blacks, and *The Second Coming* has no concern for civil rights at all. A young service station attendant who says *ax* for *ask,* the mark of many of Percy's blacks, says Will plans to send him to college. But quite to balance matters, among the furnishings in the railroad room at the old folks' home where Jack Curl presides is "A mechanical darky on a mule" who "doffed his cap" (*SC,* 310).

The civil rights movement is less controversial than before; besides, Percy has made his position clear as a Southern moderate. Yet he adds some comments about the races in the South and the nation, now that the civil rights movement has moved to a new stage: "there remains and probably there will remain a unique community in the South between black and white, so that there is much more communication, strangely enough, between middle-class white and black people in the South than there is between intellectual black and white in the North."[7]

Those remarks were made in 1973. Some years later, he said, "What has happened, of course, is that for the first time in 150 years the South and Southerners, and I mean both white and black Southerners, no longer suffer the unique onus, the peculiar burden of race which came to be part of the very connotation of the word *South.*"[8] Furthermore and finally, to make it clear: everyone has had an opinion about the South. But things have changed. "The astounding dimension of the change is that the virtues and faults of the South are the virtues and faults of the nation, no more no less. The old enemy is no longer there, or if he is, he is too busy with his own troubles. There is no one throwing punches at you and no one to counterpunch. What are you supposed to do? At least as far as writers are concerned, it does not now occur to a serious writer in the North to 'attack' the South or to a serious Southern writer to 'defend' the South."[9]

In the self-interview, he asks himself, "Can you say anything about the future of race relations?" and replies, "It's up to the blacks. The government has done all it can do. The whites' course is predictable. Like anybody else, they will simply hold on to what they've got as long as they can. When did any other human beings behave differently?

"There is a slight chance, maybe one in a hundred, that blacks and whites may learn the best of each other rather than the worst."[10]

Women

Percy shows no interest in the question of women's rights. He says,

I write about women from the exclusive point of view of the hero or anti-hero. As such, the view of women or anyone else may be limited by the narrowness of the vision. The nature of the narrowing, however, I would hope to be significant. If Binx Bolling tends to see people oddly, then perhaps the times are such that people get seen oddly. Accordingly, there is no attempt to flesh out female characters—or any other characters—in the style of the nineteenth-century novel. . . . What interests me is not how it feels to be . . . that particular woman, but how it feels to be a particular consciousness, male or female, set down in the world the way it is now. [11]

But the point may need emphasis that Percy's particular consciousnesses are men, except for Allison in *The Second Coming,* and what they are conscious of is not always particularly flattering to women.

Percy's fictional women can be divided into three groups, with several possible variants. Depressing and oppressive are the numerous old ladies, cousins, aunts, and acquired hangers on, noted for their longevity and survival, attached by kinship or other association to Southern families. They never die, and to judge by the way Percy presents them in *The Last Gentleman* they have little reason for living. Even the lady of the camellias in *Lancelot* is somewhat tainted by her resemblance to this stereotype. (Outstanding, however, and unique among classifications is staunch Aunt Emily in *The Moviegoer.*)

The two other groups are far more important. One of these is the revelers, those who lend themselves to the hump and grind of the "beastly" machine, the rape and thump that is sexual intercourse and the process of life, as Lancelot sees it. This group includes Lancelot's first wife Lucy as well as Tom's lost wife Doris and Lancelot's Margot. In short, it includes all that host of women not in either of the other groups. The third group, however, stands out also from the many nondescript and the many ill-treated females. These are the faithful wives.

Binx establishes the framework for consideration of women. Sex is for indulging, and women are to be seduced and enjoyed, like Sharon, the ripe Bama peach. This is one aspect of the sickness that he refers to as "post-Christian sex" (*M,* 207). Aunt Emily chides him for this conduct, since "gentleness with women" (*M,* 224) is one of her ideals for the Southern gentleman. His mother also quietly disapproves of his wayward fancies. The implication is that what Binx does with his women is generally welcomed by the women until they show signs of wanting to get married. Most of Percy's women are by no means models of virtue.

In *The Last Gentleman,* Percy elaborates Aunt Emily's concept of sexual conduct. And much of Will's befuddlement derives from his confusion as to what to do about sex. The question, despite Will's hesitation even to consider it and despite the slapstick associated with it, is really one of the American moral questions, having to do not merely with conduct but with family. And the matter is even more important in the South, at least for a youthful Southerner, because the South has its traditions of high ideals for women and gentlemanly conduct toward them. The situation is such that women are considered either ladies or whores and men either gentlemen or fornicators.[12] As Margot says to Lance, " 'With you I had to be either—or—but never a—uh—woman' " (L, 245). And in this novel, quite in consonance with Will's fumbling confusion is that of Kitty, a good ripe Southern plum who wishes to be whatever is expected of her. She alternates between trying to be a lady and trying to be a whore, in both cases unsuccessfully.

Causing some trouble for her is her former sister-in-law Rita, who is apparently a compassionate whore determined to be a lady by withdrawing from sexual indulgence and devoting her energies to helping mankind. This vocation is that also of the other Vaught daughter, Val, who has joined the Roman church where she may be a model of one kind of servant of God but is no longer a woman. Mrs. Vaught is a pleasant nonentity, who of course could be troublesome if another Civil War started. Mort Prince's mod daughter would presumably be willing to satisfy Will's great raging lust.

Tom (in Love in the Ruins) is capable of loving them all. In fact, women are by far his first love, though he is also capable of being devotedly monogamous. Not his capacity to love women but the loss of his daughter and difficulties with his wife have led to his sorry condition. Here, the women are hardly more than types, even his prim nurse Ellen. Moira is a dumb blonde, Lola is the embodiment of sensual potential, and Ellen is the sturdy keeper of the keys. Others include Chuck's Jewish shack-up and their hippie friend who wishes to share her chickee with Tom.

Lancelot is of course very harsh on the matter of sex. Lance's first wife played at life, which happened to include sex; Margot was unfaithful from the beginning, it seems. Even her marriage and her premarriage were aspects of her great abiding lust. She never loved, she restored. Lance's mother was either unfaithful or gave the impression so strongly as to make the truth unimportant. His daughter Lucy is ready for corruption, and Lance finds sex already appearing in the seven-year-old Siobhan. Raine is nothing but sex.

In *The Second Coming,* Kitty has become a siren, well aware of the value of her appearance and her capacity to give pleasure. She has not married a sexual performer, but she is ready to indulge, especially for a large amount of money. The thought of morality never crosses her mind, nor, possibly, does the thought of pleasure. Though Will has had a daughter by his first fat wife, neither sex nor love occurred between them during their marriage or their time together. Percy gives him a daughter to compare with other females, and this daughter is sexlessly "born-again." In fact, one aspect of *The Second Coming* is that, quite different from *Lancelot* where everyone indulged, no one ever really participates in sex until Will finds himself with Allison.

The conditions in these various novels are designed to show what Percy considers the unpleasant situation with the central concern of marriage and family. He will do what he can to repair this human condition, though he seldom succeeds in making the situation appear less than hopeless.

Ironically, each of Percy's novels is a version of the old love story, set in the novel of manners. And each has its wry version of a happy ending. Rather than merely ending another sexual encounter in recriminations and sighs, Binx deliberately takes on the ordeal of helping Kate back out of her death-in-life, a situation that seems worse than anything in the action beforehand indicated. Whatever its shortcomings, such as contrivance, a marriage occurs as this novel ends.

At the end of *The Last Gentleman,* Will is to go back to Alabama, marry Kitty, take a job as director of car salesmen, and move into the Gold Medallion Home. Percy is uncertain whether the creator of Binx Bolling ought to come so far out of the underground and participate in the society that Binx withdrew from, so he leaves the ending ambiguous. It at first seems impossible that Percy would let a character so easily accommodate himself to the ordinary. In any case, aside from the incident of Jamie's death, the important aspect of the ending of this novel is Sutter's change of view, indicated by his stopping, and the possibility of what Sutter can mean to Will. And to judge by *The Second Coming,* Percy did not plan to allow Will to return to be a proper Alabamian.

At the end of *Love in the Ruins,* though Tom has entertained ideals of honest polygamy, Tom and Ellen are married happily in their poverty. Tom has chosen Ellen, but he was also apparently deserted

by Moira and Lola, neither of whom has that sturdy frontier willingness to incorporate into a family life without a great deal of
nonsense if with some pleasure. This appears to be a genuinely
happy ending to something vaguely like a divine comedy—maybe,
that is, a human comedy of errors.

At the end of *Lancelot,* as much happens as might, under the
awesome circumstances: the action cannot realistically end with full
happiness, Lance and Anna in Virginia starting a new frontier and
a new colony, as well as new family, new life, and new republic.
Lancelot is not ready, despite his talk, and Anna is hardly ready
even after a year to submit to another man after being sexually
abused in a gang rape. Though *Lancelot* presents a wasteland in
which no salvation comes, a promise of love is made.

Finally, in *The Second Coming,* Percy appears to have found a good
woman for his good man and a man worthy of her. Will at middle
age luckily escapes the life-in-death that has long bothered him and
luckily finds a good woman, though she, Allison, has been mis-
treated, in great part by her own mother, as Will has been by his
father. They will marry and start their family by adopting old folk
as children.

Families

The large, sprawling, paternalistic Southern family is not present
in Percy's novels. Remnants of it, wherever they exist, point up the
forlorn situation of those who have no family, notably Will in *The
Last Gentleman.* Here, as with Binx and Lancelot, the old theme of
decline is treated. But this family situation is first presented immediately in *The Moviegoer.* In the first two pages, Aunt Emily is
there as last representative of a grand old past, and Scottie has just
died as first indication that Binx's immediate family is coming apart.
Binx's family finally lost its luster with his father and is currently
illuminated by a surviving uncle whose association with Southern
nobility is confined to showing his old Southern mansion to tourists
and then only because his wife had enough vim to get the idea.
Other families appear in this novel, all with difficulties that make
them less than normal. Binx's mother remarries and has a large
family, but one of the children dies and another is on the verge of
death as the novel ends. Jules Cutrere's family is there, as Aunt
Emily, a second wife, and Kate, his daughter and Emily's step-

daughter. In effect, it is no family. Harold Graebner has a baby, and that is about the extent of his life. Family life hardly exists here. With an irony that is hardly louder than a whisper, Binx says that once he and his father visited Chicago after Scott's death and at the Century of Progress stood alone "before a tableau of Stone Age Man, father mother and child" (*M,* 204).

The point about Will Barrett's family is that it does not exist. It never did. In *The Last Gentleman* no mother ever is mentioned, and in *The Second Coming* Will has a stepmother. Family is something everyone else has in the South and something therefore that Will knows about. His father has committed suicide, and the violence of that incident affects all that Will does. No more appears, and the bevy of female leftovers offers nothing. Uncle Fannin is a Southern grotesque. Will is otherwise an orphaned only child.

The Last Gentleman does have something resembling the Southern family and it is something of a family novel, in fact, but the Vaughts are used to parody that mythical family with the strong ties, the sense of community, and the community virtues. Mr. Vaught is paternalistic and generally inept, and needs someone to handle personnel matters with his wife and children as much as he does with his car salesmen. He needs someone to close any kind of deal. His wife, of course, is no manager. Rita has no authority, and one of the reasons is that the family was falling apart before she was "hired." Sutter is possessed by the too, too solid flesh in various ways. Val is lost to all but heaven, Kitty is dubiously valuable, and Jamie is a sacrifice. This is no family; it is a collection of people whom Percy wanted to use. It does have a characteristic of the Southern family in having a daughter, Myra Thigpen, from Mr. Vaught's earlier marriage who now has a solid-flesh son who always wants to know where the poontang is.

Tom's two families are fragmentary. His mother survives for no particular reason, though his father is dead and of no consequence. His daughter is dead from an ugly disease, and his wife has deserted him. Significantly, perhaps, he does appear to establish a family at the end of the novel, with a son named junior. A number of blacks in the novel who might be parents instead wander about aimlessly without families and thus are not models in that respect. Victor would make a good father, no doubt, but nothing of his family appears. Colley is married but has no children.

Lancelot's parents were separated by another kind of the death-in-life experienced by Percy's fathers. Binx's, Will's in both novels, Tom's and Lance's are all gone in some fashion. Lance's has even gone so far as to break the gentlemanly code of morality by accepting a bribe. In contrast the parents of Elgin, the intelligent young black, are alive and employed in the house. Lance's first wife is dead, and his children are all astray. Percival's parents are gone, as are Anna's.

In *The Second Coming,* Will's father haunts his memory as he attempts to find out what happened between them on the hunting field and at last rejects his father completely. Allison's parents only cause her trouble. Numerous old folks are hither and yon without ties. Will's daughter marries a Californian, but their born-again marriage promises little. It is too sophisticated on the one hand and too determinedly religious on the other. Will is estranged from this child nearly from the beginning.

And this question of the relationship between parents and children is an intense aspect of the larger situation of the family. In general, parents have no children and children no parents. What is worse, the children are injured somehow. Binx's older brother Scottie has died before the action opens, while Binx is a child. Binx's step-brother, Lonnie's older brother, whose escape to death Lonnie envies, had died before the action begins. Lonnie is suffering from a terminal disease. Will is both physically defective (he has one good ear) and mentally deficient (he has amnesia and fugues). In this novel, Jamie is more injured than Lonnie in the earlier. The naive black youth David is lost in his dreams of failing to see what the fate is for a young black in the South. In *Love in the Ruins,* Samantha's horrible disease sets off much of the action.

In *Lancelot,* a son has become homosexual, a daughter Lucy is ready to be "corrupted" in all respects, and the child Siobhan, who is apparently happy, is illegitimate. Here, finally, may be something for the future in that the black couple who have worked for Lancelot's family have an intelligent son, Elgin, who has been studying engineering at MIT and who is going to marry the girl he loves, with Lance's help, and perhaps start a family of his own. Whether Will and Allison will have a baby is not in question, since their union is more important than the issue thereof. Will's daughter was very ill when she was a child. Generally, however, parents and children are not family members in Percy's novels. Chuck, the hippie, and his father quarrel, and Chuck is thrown out of the house and into the swamp, where other homeless children live, both black and white. Will's daughter's fiancé comes in from California with his parents, curiously, since Percy thinks of Californians as being a species not elsewhere known on the earth, and he hardly expects them to have something so ordinary as families. Mort Prince's daughter endures a neglect of her own Northern kind, as do the Ohioans and Will's elevator paramour in *The Last Gentleman*. On the other hand, ironically, Chuck and his Jewish girl friend have a baby. Members of the Vaught family will not have children—except for Son, Jr., who is already there when the action begins. Jamie dies, Sutter fornicates, and Val has become sterile. Kitty will incidentally have a child for the next novel. Among the married couples in Percy's work are Nell and Eddie Lovell, whose children have grown up, the Grosses with no children, the couple who study sexual technique but have no children, and, of course, the Graebners, whose baby is specially destined for nothing. Children are maimed, and science can do nothing to help either the children or the parents. The children in Percy's novels are mostly unloved. An exception is found at the end of *Love in the Ruins*.

Chapter Four
Techniques

First-person confessional may be an appropriate term for the narrative technique in Percy's novels, though the two works dealing with Will Barrett are in the third person. All of Percy's main characters tell about their "crimes," shortcomings, and other deficiencies. Percy says he used third person in *The Last Gentleman* because Will's numerous and varied mental states would have made the novel "incoherent" if Will had been the narrator.[1] Yet he used similar distortion of sequence elsewhere, especially in *Love in the Ruins*, where Tom is also mentally awry at times. In any case, he frequently uses degrees of indirect discourse for Will's two narratives, enough to identify the narration with Will even if it is in the third person. And he uses the device of gradual recollection, the major narrative device also in *Lancelot* and perhaps intended in *Love in the Ruins* where, however, the suspense is insufficient to make the method effective. *Love in the Ruins* is nearly pure rotation for the reader. *Lancelot* is a diatribe and may be nearly pure repetition. Percy often uses versions, possibly distortions, of sequence, and these are discussed below.

And Percy often introduces dream sequences and flashbacks as narrative techniques. Particularly in *Lancelot,* where every incident is "remembered," the narrative interweaves tales of Margot's first adultery, the moviemaking that gradually involves her current adultery, recollections of his childhood and his mother's adultery along with his first marriage and his young adulthood with Percival. Here technique seems most accomplished.

The Second Coming rather effectively uses gradual recall, though the suspense is insufficient after the first reading, and the effectiveness not impressive even on first reading. *Love in the Ruins* may be a long dream sequence, beginning with the little nap on July Fourth (*LR*, 58), though something has to account for Tom's being at the intersection with his gun. His "One little catnap" ends fifteen minutes and three hundred pages later. (Percy's characters can take naps anywhere and anytime.) A long section near the end shows Tom unconscious or semiconscious with numerous characters he has known appearing to speak to him, some to tempt him to ways of life. The technique of déjà vu substitutes for stream of consciousness in a central character with no memory. It also allows identification of the last gentleman with other gentlemen, and Will represents his race like the hero of myth. A sense of boredom is associated with the idea that it has all happened before. Since Percy's main characters are usually addled, the distortions in narrative sequence suit their mental states.

All of Percy's main characters—Binx, Will in both narratives, Tom and Lancelot—are distrait. They all are wanderers if also sovereign wayfarers; and the milieu for them is always religious. But they differ little from the usual figure of the American innocent injured by experience of the world and by living in it. Their sophistication, such as it is, makes them hardly wiser about the ways of the world than a Jewish boy from Brooklyn or a youthful Southern black gone to Harlem.

Their maladjustment is signified in their own deficiencies, a tendency to inactivity and to wander, active as they may be in the search. They are disoriented. In Will's case, the disorientation is the character itself. But Tom after his attempted suicide, as well as Lancelot, spends some time in a center for aberrant behavior. Youthful acerbity in Binx, deriving from his creator, may at times conceal his "escape" to the anonymity of Gentilly where he is underground man, nibbling at society.

Percy maintains that he puts a character in a situation where, presumably, he is to live, generally through a forming ordeal. But the impression is strong that he fails to characterize sufficiently to show formation by any means, ordeal or otherwise. Enough change occurs, but not enough is there to change. And they are too much alike, generally burdened with philosophy, theology, and what is particularly characteristic of Percy's work, an anxious need to act in a hurry. The threat of something like doom remains in the background of Percy's novels. It is a vague threat and not improper perhaps, more resembling Kafka's angst than any other sense. And all of his characters are weird, in somewhat unusual situations. They resemble Southern grotesques in sensational situations. The pact

with the devil could almost come from Poe and the comic setting
for it from Mark Twain. Lancelot has sources in Hawthorne and
Erskine Caldwell. An aspect of Will comes from any Southwestern
humor column called riffraff and hayseed. Binx might almost appear
as a Young Goodman Bolling, and Lancelot is any grotesque. From
another point of view, all the characters are dreamy and romantic.

Senses

Percy does put his characters in a real world in the sense that the
properties are natural: "place, time, color, smell, and touch all
saturate the Percy style."[2] And what they sense is the world, the
flesh, and the devil. In *Lancelot*, for example, the opening pages are
dominated by references to activity of the senses, hearing and seeing,
especially in the cemetery passage where the women are quietly at
work among the dead. Lancelot emphasizes the limitations of his
"little view" through the narrow window aperture. Knowing and
perceiving are associated, especially in these opening passages,
wherein Lancelot "identifies" Percival.

As a trained pathologist and, possibly, phenomenologist, Percy
usually describes the physical appearance of his characters. In fact,
raw flesh is everywhere sufficient to suggest that Percy felt the
influence of the black humorists. Even that gentle ancient, Father
Weatherbee, is distinguished by wayward flesh, with a bleb that
blows when he speaks. Descriptions of the children's decay include
details of Samantha's neuroblastoma and her wandering eye, Jamie's
blotched skin, and Lonnie's sagging head. Kate strips her thumbs
of strings of flesh. Val feeds guts to the eagle. Will's father's brains
are scattered around the room, and in *The Second Coming* Will's wife's
fat seems to sag throughout. He even gives details of the bile that
is inaccessible through the layers of fat.

In *Love in the Ruins*, proctologists are available to treat large bowel
complaints and other fundaments and foundations associated with
these mortal coils. Tom himself is always concerned about his body.
A theme of gin fizzes and albumin molecules recurs discordantly in
the narrative that counterpoints the musical and the erotic.

In *Lancelot*, where the flesh abounds, Anna's "face was blank, lips
slightly parted and dry, like a woman asleep. She had a scar, . . .
a big white raised scar curving from forehead to cheek where she
had been cut in the rape and beating" (*L,* 109).

Possibly the best fleshly passage in all of Percy's work describes Harry Wills, who may be Lance's father, undressing after a Mardi Gras festivity: "he was oldish, blue-jowled, big-nosed, hairy-chested, strong-bellied, thin-shanked. . . . Except for his green satin helmet, sword sash, and red leatherette hip boots, he was naked. His genital was retracted, a large button over a great veined ball" (*L,* 213). The string of hyphenated adjectives is uncharacteristic of Percy (who likes them, however) and is composed of satiric epithets for a "knyght of olde," and the colors are those of a courtly lover bedight with his lady's scarves. Here also is the father with whom the hero of the heroic grail legends finds at-one-ment. Whatever Percy means in fact to suggest by this passage, it is ingenious.

Nature

Nature is the object of this concern with the senses. Percy says he cannot avoid descriptions, and he says his interest derives from his Roman Catholicism. Further, the interaction between nature and the observer is a creative activity: "Hopkins . . . thinking always that if your gaze was sufficiently fresh and if you could see it sufficiently clearly, you would see it as an act of existence, a gratuitous act of existence which was evidence of God's existence."[3] The watching and waiting he speaks of doing in his youth may have prepared him for the receptiveness and have led to the wonder he mentions in regard to Binx. In any case, his fondness for descriptions of physical nature produces excellent passages without exception and constitutes his very best writing. And some of his most adroit symbolism is associated with nature, especially with clouds and storms.

Percy is fond of using white both for descriptions of natural imagery and for symbolism. A beautiful passage, not symbol but description, appears in *The Moviegoer:* "The world is milk: sky, water, savannah. The thin etherlike water vaporizes; tendrils of fog gather like smoke; a white shaft lies straight as a ruler over the marsh. . . . The voices sound reedy and old in the wan white world." As the scene ends with two men in a boat driving away, he continues, "The hull disappears into a white middle distance and the sound goes suddenly small as if the boat had run into cotton" (*M,* 147).

Will Barrett "sniffed the morning," in *The Last Gentleman.* "It was white and dim and faraway as Brooklyn but it was a different sort of whiteness and dimness. Up yonder was a faraway Lapland sort of dimness, a public wheylike sunlight, where solitary youths carrying violin cases wait at bus stops" (*LG,* 150).

Very effective symbolism appears in the hunting scene with Will's father when Will was twelve: "A ground fog filled the hollows like milk. . . . Through the leathery leaves and against the milkiness he caught sight of a swatch of khaki . . . then could still hear the sound of the number-eight shot rattling away through the milky swamp" (*SC,* 56). Here the fog is so natural a part of the scene that its symbolism is added value. Symbolism is more explicit in another natural fog in *The Second Coming.* Here, as Will makes his way with fuddled mind to stow himself in the Confederates' hiding place, he wanders through a long limbo and a long passage that unfortunately must be excerpted and condensed.

Will looked away from the engagement party and beyond the gazebo where "A twist of cloud, thick as cotton, rose from the gorge behind the gazebo and a small scarlet oak he had never noticed before. . . . The white gazebo was almost whited out by the cloud." Will is amid puzzling out what happened in the hunting "accident" and is also planning his test for God's existence. His mind is in a particularly bad mess, and this is the cloud of his unknowing.

The cloud moves closer as Will becomes entangled: "The cloud had come over the cliff. As it came up the short steep yard it seemed to thin and turn into fog. Wisps of fog curled around the tree. . . ." As he examines the shotgun he "sighted at the windows through the barrels. White light from the cloud came spinning down the mirrored bore." As he grows more disoriented with his slices of time, "It was impossible for him to imagine entering the whited-out room tomorrow. . . . The tree was vanishing for good into the cloud," and a moment later, "The silence of the cloud seemed to press in upon the house like cotton." He decides his father was right to choose death because of life. Things get worse as Kitty approaches him again: "The room was closed up in a cloud, a white room whited out by a white cloud, but no one seemed to notice." The tree gradually vanishes. As Kitty continues, "His eyes went unfocused on the white cloud."

When he goes to the garage on the way to meet Kitty, "Tendrils of fog drifted across the clean floor." The cluster of symbols, cloud, dark scrub, tree, Kitty, Ewell with his pornographic temptation, is vaguely sexual, all expressing the erotic as Will goes to his rendezvous with God and death. As Ewell continues, "The white cloud which filled the wide doorway had grown as dense and solid as a pearl." Finally, "Ewell McBee had vanished without a trace. Swallowed up by the thick opalescent cloud." Will crosses the fence. "The cloud smelled of complex leaf rots, bark tannin and funky anise from the gorge." He settles into the cave and calls on God to "Speak . . . or be silent" and "on the following day at the height of his lunacy the cloud blew away . . . ," and his delirium begins. Meanwhile, Allison uses the "beautiful days of Indian summer" to build her negentropic system with her fantastic stove. Finally, among Will's dreams he again recalls the hunt and, "Ground fog lay straight as milk, filling the hollows between the pin oaks" (*SC*, 140–218 passim).

Percy's addiction to storms, in describing which he also shows his infinite variety, includes one here in the meeting between Will and Allison. An electrical storm occurs as they fall in love. They do not yet have sex together. "Soon the lightning was almost continuous, ripping and cracking in the woods around them. Facets of glass flashed blue and white. It was like living inside a diamond. . . . A ball of light rolled toward them down the center aisle of the greenhouse as lazily as a ball of yarn" (*SC*, 264).

In *The Moviegoer*, "The cloud is turning blue and pressing down upon us. Now the street seems closeted; the bricks of the buildings glow with yellow stored-up light" (*M*, 21). In *Lancelot* the thunder machine in the movie appears before anything else—on an October day—just before the hurricane rages along with Lance's emotions throughout the last hundred pages of the novel. "The belvedere rattled and rocked like the *Tennessee Belle*. Lightning was almost constant. A bolt hit the lightning rod. A blue light rolled along the widow's walk like a ball of yarn" (*L*, 174).

In the opening section of *Love in the Ruins*, "Far away the thunderhead, traveling fast, humps over on the horizon like a troll" (*LR*, 4). The time is five in the afternoon on the crucial July Fourth. A few pages later, are "cypresses, which are green as paint against the purple thunderhead" (*LR*, 8). And a little later, "A second thunderhead, larger and more globular, is approaching from the north. A breeze springs up. There is no thunder but lightning flickers around inside the cloud like a defective light bulb" (*LR*, 27). At seven o'clock just before he naps, he says, "Lightning flickers like a genie inside the bottle-shaped cloud" (*LR*, 56). As he dozes, "A yellow lens-shaped cloud hangs like a zeppelin over the horizon beyond the swamp" (LR, 58).

Love in the Ruins includes a passage that uses the white imagery, and contains many other delicacies: "Water is the difference! Water is the mystical element! At dawn the black bayou breathes a white vapor. The oars knock, cypress against cypress, but the sound is muffled, wrapped in cotton. As the trotline is handed along, the bank quickly disappears and the skiff seems to lift and be suspended in a new element globy and white. Silence presses in and up from the vaporish depths come floating great green turtles, blue catfish, lordly gaspergous" (LR, 382).

Two storms occur in The Moviegoer, one while Binx moves toward the meeting with Aunt Emily and another while they walk on the gallery. The sky in The Last Gentleman is filled with noxious particles, anticipating the threatening sky with the yellow cloud in Love in the Ruins. A storm bursts while Tom visits Lola at Tara, possibly intended to resemble Don Juan's descent into hell here, as Tom a second time seduces yet another girl in his erotic condition. He and Lola sit and watch the rain falling. Art Immelmann, like Mephisto, brings a storm along. (Drizzles and rains throughout do nothing for the wasteland, however.) The Bantu uprising is enhanced by the threat of storm. Uru has just announced that the blacks are taking over, when "The thunderhead fills the whole eastern sky" (LG, 140). In examples such as this, of course, the symbolism is choreographed.

Language

Language is one of Percy's dearest concerns, and with it he is nearly always excellent. James Dickey says, "I consider Mr. Percy the most original novelist now writing in English. His power of phrase is breathtaking, and is the more so because it is quiet. There is no sentence of his that does not reflect the mysterious quality of amazement that is characteristic of the poetic view of the world. Mr. Percy's fiction makes one glad that the English language is what it is, and that certain writers use it for purposes beyond any that the rest of us could ever have imagined."[4] Every word of praise is well deserved. Self-consciousness appears only in a few passages imitating Faulkner. Percy seems generally able to handle even autobiographical incidents unself-consciously.

His metaphors are rarely less than original. No matter how many clouds he talks about, he seems to find each unique. Anywhere is a good place to start. *Lancelot,* despite its unpleasant concerns, has a great many good descriptive passages, with the storms, even the artificial one, the clouds, and the bonfires on the levee. One of the best passages describes the "women in the cemetery whitewashing the tombs, trimming the tiny lawns, setting out chrysanthemums, real and plastic, lighting candles, scrubbing the marble lintels. They remind me of Baltimore housewives on their hands and knees washing the white doorsteps of row houses" (*L,* 10). "The sun was setting behind the levee and shafts of rosy light from the glazed pigeonholes pierced the dim roost like laser beams" (*L,* 28). In the next passage, which might be included above among the fleshly, he only describes what he sees:

The cheek showed the razor track of the morning's shave; above it, the demarcated swatch of light fuzz on the knoll of the cheekbone. Capillaries were rising to the surface but had not yet turned into spiders. The nose was not broken, despite football and boxing, not red, blackheaded. The eyes showed a broken vessel and a blood spot like a fertile egg. There were grains in the lashes. The hair roots were not quite clean and were dandruff-flaked. The lips were cracked. The fingernails were black. The chin showed patches of beard missed by the razor. I shaved carelessly and washed seldom. More like Ben Gunn than Lancelot. (*L,* 65)

"The soft yellow light opened like a flower and filled the room" (*L,* 233). "I turned o. my flashlight and looked at the sign in the tourist parking area. ADMISSION $5.00. A pine needle had blown through it" (*L,* 228). "A great yellow rampart of cloud filled the western sky beyond the levee. It looked as solid as the Andes and had peaks and valleys and glaciers and crevasses" (*L,* 209). "But this! How do you live with this: being stuck onto pain like a cockroach impaled on a pin?" (*L,* 209).

In *The Last Gentleman,* Percy's least poetic novel, as Will and Kitty sit beneath a billboard, "Above them, Johnnie Walker's legs creaked like ship's rigging" (*LG,* 68); "Soon the camper leapt against its tether; the wind sang like a harp in her rigging. . . . The sand scoured the aluminum skin like birdshot" (*LG,* 175). "All around them stretched a gloomy cattail swamp which smelled like a crankcase and from which arose singing clouds of mosquitoes" (*LG,* 128). ". . . his legions of *déjà vus* made everything sound familiar" (*LG,*

129). Will leaves the camper park in the camper, which "faltered and looked back of its shoulder like a horse leaving the barn. 'Not that way!—that's where I came from,' said the rider angrily and kicked the beast in the flank" (*LG, 294*).

In *Love in the Ruins,* "Her membranes are clear as light, the body fluids like jeweler's oil under a watch crystal. A lovely inorganic girl" (*LR, 92*); "I show her the snail tracks on jade, a faint cratered Fuji in a green dawn" (*LR, 93*).

Here is a metaphor from *The Last Gentleman* that some reviewer uses as an example of Percy's bad writing: "Last summer's grass was as coarse and yellow as lion's hair and worn bare in spots, exposing the tough old hide of the earth" (*LG, 4*). Maybe the extension goes too far with logic, but the *s*'s make the line sizzle with heat and dust.

Descriptions of sky appear throughout the novels. They are always impressive, and often they are brilliant. As Will prepares to service Kitty in *The Last Gentleman:* "The sky is redder. From the same direction there came a faint crepitant sound like crumpled newspaper" (*LG, 108*). And a last one from that unpoetic *Last Gentleman.* Will is at home: "It was a frosty morn. The old corn shucks hung like frozen rags. A killdeer went crying down a freshly turned row, its chevroned wing elbowing along the greasy disced-up gobbets of earth. The smell of it, the rimy mucous cold in his nostrils, and the blast of engine-warm truck air at his feet put him in mind of something—of hunting! of snot drying in your nose and the hot protein reek of fresh-killed quail" (*LG, 295*);

now the sweet ferment of alfalfa, now the smell of cottonseed meal rich as ham in the kitchen. . . . Buzzards circled, leaning into the heavy mothering air, three, four tiers of buzzards riding round a mile-high chimney of air. A shrike, the Negro's ghost bird, sat on a telephone wire and looked at him through its black mask. It was a heedless prodigal land, the ditches rank and befouled, weeds growing through the junk. . . . But across the ditches and over the turnrows . . . stretched the furrows of sifted mealy earth clean as a Japanese garden but forty miles long and going away, straight as a ruler, into the smoky distance. (*LG, 303–4*)

The passage continues for several lines. Here is the kind of thing that Percy says he would not like others to do. These are a few nearly random choices from a great many that others may prefer.

Comedy

Percy is preeminently a comic novelist and not merely because of his use of the grotesque. He was generally too earnest in *The Moviegoer,* where he hoped to please an intellectual audience with his sophisticate. Yet that novel contains what is still the best such comic scene in Percy's work. The incident occurs while Binx and Sharon are on Ship Island, after the minor accident, itself traditional comedy, has made Sharon motherly toward Binx and removed the distance between them. He has begun his attempted seduction in a rapidly moving dialogue of sweet nothings. The passage is lengthy, but as he moves quickly toward success despite the suddenness of his declaration of intent, she threatens to hit him if he advances. She assures him she can protect herself and invites him to hit her. He at last hits her "just hard enough to knock her over." "Got dog!" she says. "She gets up quickly. 'That didn't hurt. I got a good mind to hit you right in the mouth, you jackass.' "

She keeps protesting as he exaggerates his claims of love. And finally he says, " 'I can't think about anything in the world but putting my arms around you and kissing your sweet lips.' " She says,

> "Oh me."
> "Do you care if I do?"
> "I don't care if you do." (*M,* 133)

This one line of laconic capitulation is exquisite.

The sustained irony in *The Last Gentleman* makes it a comic picaresque despite its sometimes grotesque seriousness about sex and religion, apathy and purpose in life. The courteous engineer is consistently the object of satire, and only the undercurrent of dead seriousness prevents the novel from shattering the fragile tragicomedy and making it ridiculous. Serious incidents have comic undertones like the encounter in Levittown. While Will, the trained pugilist, is trying to separate actual from potential and decide whether to attack in self-defense, a woman in curlers bashes him on the nose already swollen from sinus. Much of what occurs in Shut Off and Ithaca is comedy: the hunting scene and shooting the stupid dog; the saloon gathering in Ithaca when Will knocks out the deputy; John chasing the girls. Most figures in this novel have an extra dimension in being apparently deliberate caricatures of themselves.

Tom More is also a caricature of himself, and most of what occurs with him is ironic and humorous. His pose of innocence contributes—innocent madman, innocent liberal, but *Love in the Ruins* firmly establishes the comic ability and the ability to retain the seriousness which the comedy attenuates. Even the threats that Tom invents seem real, as he consistently worries about the cloud and the end of the world. But, predictably, sexual humor, which characterizes the comedy here, is the funniest. The quiet incident with the director and the boy at the end of the pit scene, Helga and the observation room with her German accent and her curt phrases, the priest who has defrocked himself, possibly bisexual, consoling himself at a vaginal console, Lola on her horse with her gun, the figure of Moira, obsessed with flappers and thinking Montovani classical, Art Immelmann patting himself as a last grooming action, the idea that all the mishaps are the work of a madman, the large bowel complaint—the list is endless.

It may be fortunate that Percy established his comic ability before he wrote *Lancelot* and *The Second Coming,* though this last somber novel contains numerous comic episodes. *Lancelot* is too mean. Will in *The Second Coming* is too earnest and too poor spirited to be funny even when ridiculous. The courtship of Margot in *Lancelot,* lasting for two drinks and thirty minutes, is comparatively light. Margot's restoration and her attempts to furnish a business office and study into which to fit Lance as an incarnation of Jefferson Davis are, of course, traditional comedy of character. Uncle Harry as well as Lancelot's father and mother are comic figures in their grotesqueries, vaguely like Chekhovian characters. The idiocies of the townspeople over the movie stars is satire. Such incidents of comedy, however, are generally lost in the extremes of the narrative.

The approach in these last two novels gives relevance to some remarks Percy made in mid-career to an interviewer, who suggested that "comedy for its own sake" was "a kind of nihilistic play." Percy replied,

That is what is wrong with the American so-called black comedy: absurd situation for its own sake, gags, impossible situations. . . . I deplore this. I think that using black comedy for the sake of itself defeats art. But, you know, I think I owe a good deal of the kind of humor that I use to Jewish humor, which is a very wry, self-critical sort of humor. . . . I think I find myself using what the Jewish comedians call the gag—a one-liner. And there again we have the same situation: Jewish humor developing from an oppressive and tragic situation. We were talking about the common fact of black humor being connected with a difficult situation. Surely there is a connection there, too, of humor in a difficult situation. Kafka's sharp, devastating humor certainly traces back to ghetto literature. I am reading Böll now. The relationship of religion and humor is interesting. He is a German Roman Catholic and uses the most devastating satirical humor, often extremely anti-clerical. I find a kinship with him. I find it perfectly natural for a Catholic writer to fall into this harsh, satirical comic technique.

He adds that what interests him is "humor used in the service of satire. . . . There is no more deadly weapon."[5]

The date of this interview is 1974, which makes it fall midway between publication of *Love in the Ruins* and *Lancelot*. These views may account for the harsh treatment of Percival and, later, of the priest Jack Curl in *The Second Coming*. Occasional one-liners seem to be intended in this latter novel. Something approaching black comedy characterizes the tone of both. In any case, among the numerous incidents in *The Second Coming,* Will's ridiculous intent to force God's hand by holing up in the cave is the most elaborate stunt in Percy's work, surpassing Tom's salvation machine, Will's trek cross country to require of Sutter the unfolded mystery, and Lancelot's plan to begin a third revolution.

Kitty cuts the most ridiculous figure, though. Her fistfighting attack on Will is amusing to the old men just before they have their own joust among the pillows. Kitty's husband, with all his prejudices, is a droll comedian, possibly based on television's Archie Bunker. Allison's first lover is something of a comic figure. Jack Curl, as the fat friar, is one of the traditional figures in comedy. Father Weatherbee is comical in appearance, and he shows a good stern sense of humor himself in comparing Jack Curl with the dung bird. A touch of black humor probably appears in Marion's fat and her attachment to funerals and food. Both Ewell McBee and Jimmy Rogers have special seriocomic roles. While *Love in the Ruins* seems like the best traditional comedy and satire among Percy's novels, his last novel may be the most complex in that mode.

Chapter Five
The Moviegoer

The Moviegoer is an episodic first-person *récit* by John Binkerson ("Binx") Bolling, the first of Percy's Southerners of good family and impressive names. The novel is a somewhat pretentious edifying discourse, in part because the narrator is so decisive in his numerous opinions. He enjoys even bad movies, at which he spends much of his time because he has nothing else to do except make money and seduce his secretaries. With money and sex as his interests, he is the typical materialistic American businessman, an informed consumer, and a producer. But he finds himself ill-attuned. The narrative covers the week of Mardi Gras, a carnival of life, ending on Ash Wednesday, a day of contrition, when the mark is put on the flesh. On this occasion just before the start of Lent, Christians are having their most indulgent week of holidays. This is also the week of Binx's thirty-first birthday, the age of adulthood and ordeal for the traditional hero. The time has come for vague stirrings in the soul and for knights to take up quests.

Binx awoke, he says, with an intuition of the search, a concept only vaguely defined in the action, though it seems to refer to realization of the self by a search for place that allows a man to make what Binx calls a "little contribution" to society. While the quest does not end with Binx's conversion, it may end with a personal religious experience. Here, as in the myth of the hero that vaguely informs the action, a search for the father occurs. In Binx's case, the father is an alienated Southern romantic whose antics led him to joyful heroic death during World War II. These alienated spirits, father and son, have related maladies, though the novel intends only to show a gradual decline in commitment to decisive activity, as mores and morals grow dissolute in the twentieth century.

Binx's Aunt Emily, a stoical Southern noblewoman, has some idea about what Binx should do with his wasted getting and spending, and he begins the narrative by saying he has a note from her containing an unexpected invitation to luncheon on a Wednesday. Breaking her own habit means she will wish to discuss either his "cousin" Kate's mental health or his own future. Kate's health and Binx's future are the main concerns of the narrative and the ostensible reason for Binx's storytelling. Much of the remaining content is satiric irony about American culture, with its emphasis on technology, and the failure of scientific humanism in a world devoid of values. The tone during most of the narrative is that of a detached sophisticate who deprecates the materialistic niceties in which he indulges, though Binx may also intend to present himself as a genuine and consenting product of the culture.

With this intuition of a search, Binx becomes involved in a version of the call made upon the hero to be up and doing. He feels the Shadenfreude, the combined joy and fear, that often affects Percy's characters. An epilogue to the action resolves the difficulties. Binx and Kate are married and joined in a long partnership, for better or worse, and Binx is in medical school, at last preparing for a profession as his acquaintances have urged him to do and ready to perform in society rather than withdrawing. What he will contribute is a theme of the epilogue, discussed below.

Alienation and Conformity

The narrative presents the situation that has led Binx to become a bond salesman who moved out of the French Quarter, with what he considers its excessive and diverse sexual indulgence—"Birmingham businessmen smirking around Bourbon Street and the homosexuals and patio connoisseurs on Royal Street" (*M*, 6)—to live in Mrs. Schexnaydre's basement, at the bottom of life, in Gentilly where he is a genially indifferent and unsocial animal enjoying the accomplishments of a uniform technological society. He lives his "secret existence among the happy shades in Elysian Fields" (*M*, 99). He has let national advertising of products keep him smelling good, for example; and *Consumer Reports* makes his decisions about creature comforts. He is precisely a creature who has little physical distinction from the crowd, whatever his unconscious awareness of his inactive slumber. Percy says, "Binx enjoys his alienation. He is happy in what Kierkegaard calls the aesthetic mode—he lives in a place like Gentilly to savor its ordinariness."[1] He enjoys both the use of Christendom and the criticism of it.

As the narrative moves through events of the week, it tells of Kate's vague difficulties, brought on in great part apparently because of her fiancé's sudden death some years before in an automobile accident but also by the malaise of a poor little rich girl with nothing to do. She has even tried social work and good deeds generally, but she is of little faith even at the end of the action. Percy says, however, that he intended to "portray the rebellion of two young people against the shallowness and tastelessness of modern life. The rebellion takes different forms. In Kate, it manifests itself through psychiatric symptoms: anxiety, suicidal tendencies and the like. In Binx it is a 'metaphysical' rebellion—a search for meaning which is the occasion of a rather antic life in a suburb of New Orleans."[2] He wishes, that is, to show the deficiencies of that comfortable humanism that no longer concerns itself with either Christianity or individuality. He also says he intended a dialectic between the stoic view, a basically pessimistic emphasis on a moral code without a belief in God, as practiced by the nobility of the South and by others who depend more upon man than on God; and on the other hand, traditional Roman Catholic ease with both morality and religion. And he adds a third theme: "the protagonist is in an existentialist predicament, alienated from both cultures."[3]

For the dialectic, Percy creates a forceful Aunt Emily, avatar of his own "Uncle Will," to present eloquently the case for persisting in the performance of one's duty, a code that she urges upon the capable Binx, whose family has furnished doctors and lawyers to society throughout its history. And Binx's remarried mother's large family, the anonymous Smiths rather than the distinguished Bollings, seen at their fishing camp, represent the practice of habitual and unexamined religion. Among the varied forms of Roman worship is that of the wealthy and unconcerned Uncle Jules. But wishing to make Roman Catholicism more than the casual habit of attending Sunday Mass, or discussing the schedule for it, Percy invents a sickly teenage stepbrother, named Lonnie, devout and conscientious, possibly intended as a sacrificial figure, whose death at the end of the book dramatizes the Christian promise and perhaps existential significance of individual death. Lonnie's theologizing somewhat counteracts Aunt Emily's philosophizing about human valuelessness, at least in presenting the orthodox concepts of Roman Catholics and specifically a belief in God. Religion is distinctly a theme in the novel.

The Shades of Elysian Fields

Binx says early in the action that he has lately got the impression that everyone is dead. He, too, is dead presumably until he wakes with an intuition of the search and realizes that something is missing. This novel may intend to suggest that God is what is lacking, but it does not until possibly near the end. The point made is of the negativity, the lack. Among the dead are Sam Yerger and his wife, artist cosmopolites, nonmoral beautiful people, whose view of the good life probably conceals their despair. A young Jewish couple named Gross, not quite in refined society, as the name suggests, represent the enterprising business element of society, content with making money. Kate's current fiancé, Walter, a lawyer, is the kind of professional man, member of the club, vaguely dissatisfied because the halcyon college and fraternity life is gone, who never will know what a quest is.

On a train ride to Chicago and a bus ride back to New Orleans, trips designed to illustrate Percy's concepts of rotation and repetition, respectively adventure and rediscovery, future and past, other types appear. Among them is a youthful romantic who will never know what to do with himself, like Binx's father. A man from St. Louis clips instructive articles to file away for reference in dealing with life's situations. He is especially concerned with an item that deals not with life but with attempts at combining social and physical sciences designed to study and explain all human behavior and all problems, including those of the spirit. One among the group is a genuinely enthusiastic and uncomplicated salesman who accepts the values of technology as accomplishments that alleviate man's fate and decrease his labor while aiding him to operate in nature's garden.

Nell and Eddie Lovell, Harold Graebner and his wife, and the sex therapists, some of the numerous couples in this novel, along with the blacks, are the real inhabitants of this dead land. As Binx talks with Eddie, he realizes that "family projects, lovely houses, little theater readings" (M, 18) are the events of living for most of these bourgeoisie. Nell later tells him she and Eddie have "reexamined their values and found them pretty darn enduring" (M, 101). They have spent an evening playing records and reading *The Prophet* aloud by the fire. Harold Graebner is a nondescript businessman with nothing but money acquired from an inherited business that just grows and a baby that perpetuates the human condition. As the soldier who saved Binx in Korea, he was for a brief moment a complete and instinctive hero who, however, seems to have had no idea that his action led him for a short time to life. Binx's reappearance now is a threat to the couple's stability and everyday insularity. Mercer, the butler, represents the aspiring blacks, living an inauthentic life somewhere on the edge of the middle class, and trying pathetically as a Rosicrucian to discover his secret powers so he can get out of his helpless condition of servitude and tyrannize over others. He and the Lovells with their *Prophet*—neither capable of being religious—cultivate these weak substitutes for being. Worse for the Negroes, they consciously attempt to imitate the dispirited whites and acquire their valueless manners.

Everydayness and Malaise

Binx is afflicted with a mordant world-weariness, strikingly like that of the romantics, that he refers to variously as the malaise and everydayness. The malady resembles Baudelaire's ennui as well as what Kierkegaard calls despair and whatever Camus's Meurseult endures. Everydayness is the drag of uneventful, unchallenging life for those living in an environment so successful in satisfying physical needs that it encourages a man to be a content animal uninterested in either this world or the next. Malaise is the name of the disease of depression and despair, intensified by the awareness of a moral and metaphysical wasteland in which intellectuals claim to have outgrown the rituals and beliefs of organized religion and "believe in people . . . tolerance and understanding . . . the uniqueness and the dignity of the individual" (*M*, 109). These are the non-believers whom Will includes in his litany for the dead in *The Second Coming*. The disease deprives life of any semblance of adventure and purpose, and the values are mere impracticable abstractions. Precisely, however, individuality is lacking in the styrene society where all experience is packaged and wrapped, as Percy describes it in "The Loss of the Creature," an essay in his collection of philosophical essays called *The Message in the Bottle*.

But as Binx explains the problem, his affliction is an inability characteristic of Western man, or at least of the Western intellectual, to keep body and soul together in a harmony sufficient to allow him to act reasonably in the concrete world of objects and other people. He has the experience of what he calls a vertical search, climaxed when he read in an anonymous hotel room *Chemistry of Life,* which in a sense asks, or answers, the ultimate question as to what life is made of. Ironically, however, the book deals not with what it is to live and have being but with the chemicals of living and of life's beginnings in nitrogen, oxygen, carbon, and methane. It deals with the life that the physical scientist studies. Chemical life has nothing to do with being, either at the sublime level where the question is how something comes from nothing or at the mundane level where the problem is how to get along from day to day in a world that often seems absurd. Binx says that when he finished reading this and other books produced by the world of scientific humanism, he discovered the world was accounted for but that he was himself left over as a particular individual man living somewhere. What was he to do with the rest of his life? This is the problem for all of Percy's characters. Four o'clock in the afternoon seems to be their most miserable hour.

With this experience in awareness, Binx then began what he calls his horizontal search. Both terms are derived from Kierkegaard's "The Difference between a Genius and an Apostle,"[4] which provided Percy with a distinction that he later used to dramatize the significance of the priestly messenger bearing the Good News. The horizontal search is that of a man combining existentialism and phenomenology, someone attempting to live from day to day in the real physical world of nature and men rather than in a world of dreams, utopias, or abstractions, where the challenge of life vanished as physical wants were gradually satisfied. He will attempt to live daily in the concrete world where a man is also a product of the world among other men in physical nature. He will attempt to avoid the abstract, the impulse to deal with statistics and averages and packaged experience and avoid being an anyone anywhere. Now, he says, he has begun to live. He searches for his origins and lives "solitary and in wonder" (*M,* 42), wonder about the mysteries and marvels of the natural universe, fascinated by the diversity of creation and bored by the humanistic verities.

Moviegoing

Moviegoing has several functions in this novel, most of them ultimately unsuccessful.[5] Binx says that he likes even bad movies, though he gives no examples of movies he thinks bad. What he particularly likes were the scene in *Stagecoach* when John Wayne kills three men as he falls and the scene in *The Third Man* when the kitten finds Orson Welles in the doorway. The first of these incidents is absurd if Binx is interested in reality, whatever may be said of the dramatic suspense with the cat and Orson Welles. Moviegoing provides patterns for behavior, though it is of dubious value in so doing. Binx says, for example, that he is no "do-gooding Jose Ferrer" (*M*, 74), a reference that is in effect a metaphor. Sharon in some action resembles Joan Fontaine, and Kate once resembles a character played by Eva Marie Saint. A man on the train resembles the actor Gary Merrill, a different kind of metaphor, its significance depending on whether the reader knows what the actor looks like.

On several occasions, Binx says he is posing as a particular movie star, usually in his attempt to seduce Sharon. At one time or another he gestures like Gregory Peck, Dana Andrews, and Clark Gable. He of course mentions Rory Calhoun and Tony Curtis as well as "Bill Holden, my noble Will" (*M*, 127), but these stars are something more than role models. In fact, as noted below, he is never able to act like them, because he fails before he attains their "resplendent reality" (*M*, 16).

Generally, the moviegoing is associated with concepts that in interviews Percy ascribes to Kierkegaard. During the week, hardly a typical one, surely, for moviegoing, Binx sees at least four movies, samples a fifth (with Jane Powell) and watches a television "play" with Dick Powell. With the movies he associates a concept that presumably eases his alienation, though he never says as much.

The first movie he sees on Wednesday night after the depressing visit with Aunt Emily and Kate. It is *Panic in the Streets,* with Richard Widmark, one of those typically sensationalist horrors dealing with "a cholera bacilli . . . gotten loose in the city" (*M*, 63). Title and star are unimportant, as is the case with most of the movies Binx mentions. But the movie is associated with "a phenomenon of moviegoing": seeing the city on film allows the moviegoer "to live, for a time at least, as a person who is Somewhere and not Anywhere" (*M*, 63). This appears to be a final crucial step in recovering from alienation. The next movie he sees is associated with a related concept. On Thursday as he walks home to Gentilly Binx stops at a theater where Jane Powell is playing in a musical. He is not interested, but here he takes the trouble to talk about knowing the manager and the cashier and to explain that he tries to get some facts: "Before I see a movie it is necessary for me to learn something about the theater or the people who operate it" (*M, 74*). "If I did not," he says, "I should be seeing one copy of a film which might be shown anywhere and at any time" (*M, 75*). All this talk of attempt to fix oneself somewhat helps to make the doctrine of certification plausible, but aside from the dull facts given in this long passage the matter is not otherwise discussed in the novel. The theme is of course one of the major themes of the novel and of the essays in *The Message in the Bottle*. But such mundane information is not given in regard to any of the other movies, certainly not to the "Aztec mortuary" movie house in Chicago far from his own neighborhood. But, finally, when the idea of certification in the face of potential anonymity receives all the attention it deserves, who ever has the chance to go to the movie and get his neighborhood certified? How many back lots in Hollywood can certify somebody's Main Street?

Somewhat later at home on Thursday, Binx sees a television movie starring Dick Powell in one of his serious roles. It is very much like an ordinary movie, with a sentimental resolution, to which, however, he attaches no philosophical burden. Presumably, he merely spends time while waiting for Kate, having nothing else to do after he reads the article Mrs. Shexnaydre has clipped from *Reader's Digest*. Later in the evening, he goes with Kate to see yet another movie, where he has what he calls "a successful repetition" (*M, 79*). He mentions *The Oxbow Incident* and *All Quiet on the Western Front* as being associated with the idea that "All movies smell of a neighborhood and a season" (*M, 79*), a phenomenological remark, presumably, that makes no real sense, though he gives examples. The occasion of this movie, however, is to define repetition, which he does very ambiguously, though later references in interviews and earlier ones in "The Man on the Train" appear to give the word and concept the usual definition. He says, "A repetition is the reenactment of past experience toward the end of isolating the time segment which has lapsed in order that it, the lapsed time, can be savored of itself and without the usual adulteration of events that clog time like peanuts in brittle" (*M, 79–80*). He reemphasizes this concentration on the span of time by rhetorically asking at the end of the paragraph, "How, then, tasted my own fourteen years since *The Oxbow Incident*?" And he replies that among other things there was "a secret sense of wonder about the enduring . . . alone in the empty theater. The enduring is something which must be accounted for" (*M*, 80). Well. Is he talking about the lapsed time—about time itself with the associated concept of endurance? Or is he, as always seems the case in the interviews, talking about reexperiencing the same or similar content? As he waits on this Thursday evening, he speaks of "the homeliest of repetitions," which is listening "every night at ten to a program called This I Believe" (*M*, 108). He describes sensations on seeing another Western at the same place as if they were important. And he does define repetition as "re-enactment of past experience" (*M*, 80). In any case, the movie itself has no importance except that with the repetition, whatever the experience was, both movies were Western. "The Man on the Train" mentions the Western as presenting the relationship of stranger, potential, timing, and actuality that makes the perfect rotation (*MB*, 93–94).

An apparently important episode is the visit to a drive-in with Lonnie, Sharon, and some of the younger children to see *Fort Dobbs*. Here is where Binx defines rotation. (Possibly to the point, this is the first date with Sharon as well as occasion of their moviegoing together and also the last. She is the last of a long line of aesthetic, or sexual, rotations). Here the experience is beyond his expectations, he says. Clint Walker is impressively Western and solitary, with the perfect lingual gesture, Lonnie is pleased, and Sharon is being like a girl in the movies who will allow her man sexual pleasure with her because he is kind to children. The only time Binx had a better similar experience was when he saw another movie, not when enjoying sex with Sharons or Lindas. All this is designed to define rotation, and nothing is said here about knowing owners or cashiers at movie houses.

Binx says, "A rotation I define as the experiencing of the new beyond the expectation of the experiencing of the new" (*M*, 144). And the idea, to judge from Percy's essays, is to make an unexpected discovery in the physical world. Then Binx says, "The only other rotation I can recall which was possibly superior was a movie I saw before the war called *Dark Waters*." The stars, Thomas Mitchell and Merle Oberon, "drive into the village—to see a movie! A repetition within a rotation. I was nearly beside myself with rotatory emotion" (*M*, 144). Now this is sheer superciliousness from a lonely narrator and writer with more to hide from the reader than convey to him. Binx is not elsewhere the kind of person to gush in this manner. This cannot be joy. It also cannot be a repetition either by ordinary definition or by the incomprehensible one Binx gives earlier. For the stars go to the movie. Binx does not, and merely going to the movie is not even a rotation, so far as we certainly know. Further, here is a perfect case in which a book might have served quite as well as a movie, which means that the narrative is what matters and not the medium. "The movies are onto the search, but they screw it up" (*M, 13*), Binx says elsewhere. The movies screw it up because the movies are no good, which is true of most books also, especially in the fifties, when movies were not much onto the search at all.

A hint of the meaning of moviegoing appears in the account of the young romantic on the bus who "is a moviegoer, though of course he does not go to the movies" (*M, 216*). That is, he is obviously a silly little boy who does not know how to act. So he always will act like someone else if he is lucky. If he is unlucky, he will always act silly, wondering what to do next, unable to play a role, and without a self to act like.

Presumably the more a moviegoer attends the movies, the more intense is his awareness of the abyss beneath him, a cavity that develops in great part because he has ceased to live in the world of being and significance and has withdrawn into the abstract, tidy but unchallenging world of scientific humanism. If he were really living he would not be at the movies at all, using theaters as places. And movies would not represent the *limits of his imagination,* as moviegoing does.

But the people in the movies know what to do. They are real and not anonymous. They are in fact so much themselves that they play themselves rather than acting in roles. Movie stars are one with themselves individually while they perform. If they endure anomie or identity crises, the difficulty is required in the plot. They are preferable to life. The roles are designed for them to perform with the gestural perfection that Percy mentions in "The Man on the Train." They do not have to wonder what to do, where to live, what role to take, when to use deodorant and credit cards. Or what to do with time. They do not even sweat or buy on credit, and they no doubt always curl up with something absorbing at four o'clock on Thursday afternoons. They do not have to bother about living from day to day. Writers, producers, directors establish them in a celluloid world and laminate them in plastic. They never fail to do the "right" thing, the gesturally perfect thing, the thing the script demands. They do not speculate. They act. Even if the "wrong" thing is done, it too is done perfectly, according to the director's rationale for acting alienated like Binx or bemused like Will. Rory Calhoun, Tony Curtis, and other movie heroes Binx mentions are then not ideals or heroes but people to imitate in the process of living from day to day in ordinary interpersonal situations. They know how to act, and they always act properly. They have happy endings and exciting lives. They perform sexually and as lovers, and they are models beyond reach. Their heightened lives give life its resplendent reality, make living seem easy and quick. They do the living for someone who lives in the land of the dead. They do Binx's living for him because he cannot live for himself. This precisely is the reason he calls upon the god Rory when flesh fails him at his one fleshly trial.

But, after all, these movies and these stars have no value. Twenty years later, being "Gregory Peckorish" has no meaning (except for the sexual pun on the name). Going to movies has no meaning. Percy may have counted on his references to Rory and Tony to introduce and emphasize the sexual that, despite Binx's references to his line of seductions, never reveals its importance to Percy (and Binx) even after the failure with Kate and the apostrophe to Rory. The concepts of rotation and repetition may of course have their uses as techniques in storytelling, whatever their use in alleviating alienation.

Desire and Despair

Binx's excessive concern with his prejudices, feelings, and definitions nearly conceals a major theme of the novel, introduced quite early in the monologue and resolved only in the epilogue. The distinction between love and sex that occupies Percy throughout his work only gradually emerges in *The Moviegoer* in Binx's ordinary remarks about unsatisfied sexual longings. Excessive concern with the sickly and sexless Kate and relatively short exaggerated episodes with Sharon as well as narrative serenity conceal, or fail to reveal, Binx's falling prey to "desire" (*M*, 228). He of course outlines his series of affairs and talks of his dedication to the flesh. His description of the girl on the bus with the Prince Val bangs who is wrapped in cellophane like a gift from the world hints at the kind of joy Tom More feels and that Will Barrett moans for. Binx says his desire for Sharon is like a "sorrow in my heart" (*M*, 68). He anticipates Sutter's idea that sex is the only mode of reentry into the concrete world. When Binx's mother says her father liked pretty girls "Till his dying day," Binx says, "Does it last that long?" (*M*, 155).

But Kate's role, occupying long, dull portions of the narrative, otherwise intrusive and unclear, clarifies upon recognition of the importance of this theme. On one level, Kate is a type of the harrassed heroine of Southern fiction, resembling a character from Tennessee Williams, specifically Carol Cutrere in *Battle of Angels.* While characterization is relatively unimportant, she appears as bifurcated schizophrenic, sometimes calm and efficient and sometimes so ill that she is nearly helpless. Though the theme is muted, she is associated with the theme of lady and whore, anticipating Kitty in *The Last Gentleman,* alternately innocent and bold, Doris in *Love in the Ruins* and Margot in *Lancelot.* Finally, she thinks she ought to indulge with Binx on the train, in great part apparently because she thinks sex is what he wants of her. Here she acts like a whore and Binx must treat her like a lady. No wonder he calls for Rory, patron saint. But he shifts quite on his own from his Lindas and Sharons to Kate and back.

The most specific and unexpected statement about the theme comes later when Binx and Kate are on the way to visit the Graebners and "pass within a few feet of noble Midwestern girls with their clear eyes and their splendid butts and never a thought for them" (*M*, 207). Why? He has just finished confessing to Rory Calhoun that he failed in the sexual episode with Kate in her boldness. He sounds like Tom. But he goes on, and at last the point is made:

What a sickness it is, Rory, this latter-day post-Christian sex. To be pagan it would be one thing, an easement taken easily in a rosy old pagan world; to be Christian it would be another thing, fornication forbidden and not even to be thought of in the new life, and I can see that it need not be thought of if there were such a life. But to be neither pagan nor Christian but this: this is sickness, Rory. For it to be longed after and dreamed of the first twenty years of one's life, not practiced but not quite prohibited; simply longed after, longed after as a fruit not really forbidden but mock-forbidden and therefore secretly prized, prized first last and always by the cult of the naughty nice wherein everyone is nicer than Christians and

naughtier than pagans, wherein there are dreamed not one but two American dreams. (*M*, 207)

Presumably, he means he was unable to treat Kate like an object
of desire, thus cannot perform with her until they are married.
Actually, he will not, because this precisely is Percy's wish: to point
to marriage as the prerequisite for sexual intercourse.

In view of what happens in the rest of Percy's work, this passage
is about the most important in *The Moviegoer,* because its subject is
so closely associated with the despair—the vague wish for death or
escape. Binx's marriage then is the most significant event in the
novel, not because he devotes himself to Kate, or not that ordeal
alone, for he has loved her for some time, but because he gives up
sex for love or at least engages in marriage and accepts that institution's responsibilities. Binx is not alienated because of desire,
though. Percy uses the alienation to preach about sexual morality.
And the ending of the book is as significant as the endings of the
other novels. Here is such ideal as may emerge from this despair of
both Binx and Kate. While Binx may begin his ordeal, he begins
with serious hope, and the ending is a happy one. Kate herself may
come to something, ex nihilo, as she chooses marriage, leaps to
faith, and accepts "shared consciousness,"[6] an ideal in intersubjectivity that Percy discussed in, among other places, the essay, "The
Symbolic Structure of Interpersonal Process."

The Little Way

Percy makes several comments about the outcome of the narrative:
"The ending is ambiguous. It is not made clear whether he returns
to his mother's religion or takes on his aunt's stoic values. But he
does manage to make a life by going into medicine, helping Kate
by marrying her."[7] Yet Percy elsewhere makes remarks that appear
to say that Binx "regained his mother's religion" though "what he
believes is not the reader's business."[8] And he tells Carr, "Binx,
who exists in the aesthetic mode of damnation, as Kierkegaard would
call it, in the end becomes a believer, in his own rather laconic
style."[9]

Percy adds one other observation to these remarks: "But in the
end—we're using Kierkegaardian terminology—in the end Binx
jumps from the esthetic clear across the ethical to the religious. He
has no ethical sphere at all. That's what Aunt Emily can't understand

about him. He just doesn't believe in being the honorable man, doing the right thing, for its own sake."[10] The aesthetic here refers not to the beautiful but to the experience of the senses, both seeing, for example, and touching—with special reference to sex. The ethical refers in this context to the humanistic practice of good conduct with, or more likely without, a belief in God.

Several ideas are important here. This matter of good conduct and its relationship to a belief in God is the ageless question whether a man can accomplish anything by being good without being Christian. The Christian church of course replies that he cannot. Good works without faith are of no value. Binx has, then, already rejected Aunt Emily's values, as he tells her when she lectures him about his presumed sexual misconduct with Kate on the train. He does not necessarily mean that her values are absolutely worthless but that they are simply insufficient. When Percy says Binx does not wish to be the honorable man, he means by implication that Binx refuses to be the honorable man alone and not also the Christian. And what religion he would have chosen would of course not be in doubt, since the writer is a Roman Catholic writer. Actually, however, Binx has not been dishonorable or unethical except in his affairs of the heart. This action is of course unchristian, and to some extent wrong in Aunt Emily's opinion, since gentleness to women is important in her moral code and in that of the fallen paradise of Mississippi.[11] But, finally, however, the action only implies that Binx has jumped to the religious stage, if literal practice is a mark of what has occurred. The action shows him only with a revised moral code.

No doubt he is on the point of becoming both a doctor and a Christian. He has married so that sex is legal, and he is preparing to serve. He even uses the word *vocation:* "There is only one thing I can do: listen to people, see how they stick themselves into the world, hand them along a ways in their dark journey and be handed along, and for good and selfish reasons. It only remains to decide whether this vocation is best pursued in a service station or—" (*M,* 233) the implication being presumably that this code applies in any vocation.

The selfish reasons presumably apply to his soul's welfare, his salvation, eternal life. He seems to be talking about a Christian community. He will work for his own sake with others without abstractions about human dignity but with devotion to personal salvation. He will avoid being "an anyone, a warm and creative person" (M, 228), in the humanistic utopia. About his search, he says, "I have not the authority, as the great Danish philosopher declared, to speak of such matters in any way other than the edifying" (M, 237). He has no authority to deliver the Christian message, no authority to evangelize, really. The reference is to Kierkegaard's distinction between genius and apostle. Binx has no authority to deliver the Good News or to discuss matters of truthseeking and God's grace, since he is not appointed to that role and not ordained as an official in the church. The genius can speak of human truth, as a scientist does of laws. But he who speaks of divine truth must be one whom the church through God has ordained and appointed to that purpose. Binx's idea of putting "a foot in the right place as the opportunity presents itself" (M, 237) may be a little too personal for the occasion here.

Yet amid these preoccupations, Binx deals with two beautiful scenes. Whatever the ambiguity of the passage dealing with the black man who comes to the Ash Wednesday service, the observations leave room for possibilities. First, Binx asks whether the man is there because it is "part and parcel of the complex business of coming up in the world? Or is it because he believes that God himself is present here on the corner of Elysian Fields and Bons Enfants? Or is he here for both reasons: through some dim dazzling trick of grace, coming for the one and receiving the other as God's own importunate bonus?" (M, 235). These words are those of a religious man, even if they may come from the author and not the character. The black may be climbing realistically to the level of the white middle class, unconcerned that the black cross will hardly show on his dark forehead. But no matter. God is there.

The other scene is a narrative of the reaction to Lonnie's death, later amplified in the account of Jamie's baptism at his death. Kate's overwrought reaction contrasts with that of Binx and the children. Hers is a humanist reaction, in fact, not a Christian one. Binx is unconcerned with Lonnie's color or the pity of it but with the dignity of Lonnie's death and with his truthful remark that he had "conquered an habitual disposition" (M, 239) to envy his older brother who had died.

Finally, the scene with the children parallels the scene briefly described in the second paragraph of the novel. Aunt Emily tells Binx that Scottie is dead and says, " 'I know you're going to act like a soldier' " (*M,* 4), like a stoic not a Christian. When Scottie died, Binx was to show no reaction to an event that for existentialists makes life meaningful and individualistic. But Binx shares their experience of Lonnie's death with the children and says Lonnie "wouldn't want you to be sad. He told me to give you a kiss and tell you that he loved you" (*M,* 239). Lonnie was anointed and "When our Lord raises us up on the last day . . . he'll be able to ski" (*M,* 240). Here is the hope.

Purpose

The accomplishment of this novel is that it is almost not a failure, despite its numerous shortcomings. But it was written, whatever Percy's theories about didacticism and art, to display ideas outlined mostly in the essay "The Man on the Train," which was published in 1956 and deals with the subject of alienation. (Percy himself somewhere says he finally found a vehicle to express his ideas.) In "The Man on the Train," he theorizes insistently that art can reverse alienation, especially through the literary (and presumably lifelike) devices of repetition and rotation. He cites Kafka's work as an accomplished example of what the suffering artist can do to relieve his own alienation through communication, by providing an inter-subjective relationship between artist and reader through the written work. No specific outlines appear in that essay, but the following remarks (taken from a much longer passage) strongly hint at what occurred.

The modern literature of alienation is in reality the triumphant reversal of alienation through its re-presenting. It is not an existential solution . . . but is an aesthetic victory of comradeliness, a recognition of plight in common. . . . A literature of rotation . . . is . . . one mode of escape from alienation. Its literary re-presenting does not change its character in the least, for it is, to begin with, the category of the New. . . . But what is notable about it for our purposes, this quest for the remote, is that it is peculiarly suited to re-presenting; it transmits through art without the loss of a trait. As a mode of deliverance from alienation, experiencing it directly is no different from experiencing it through art. (*MB,* 93)

The wish to illustrate, and even try out, these theories explains the studied definitions of repetition (the "quest for the remote"?), rotation, and certification, the latter discussed in yet another essay, "The Loss of the Creature," published in 1958. Here again is a practical reason for the movie references in *The Moviegoer*. Percy speaks to the alienated not only in the language he knew well from attending movies consistently but also in the allusions they will recognize, not literary allusions but allusions to the movies and movie stars of the date of publication of the novel, 1960.

In another essay, "Notes for a Novel about the End of the World," published some years later, he remembers an idea obviously associated with Binx: The novelist, he says, "sketches out a character, a businessman-commuter, who, let us say, is in some sense or other *lost* to himself. That is to say, he feels that something has gone badly wrong in the everyday round of business activity. . . . Even though by all objective criteria all is well with him, he knows that all is not well with him" (*MB,* 108). Only this particular statement of the idea is unique; the idea itself appears in "The Man on the Train," before Percy began writing novels. The idea of a commuter may be retained in Binx's preference for buses over cars and may account for the train and bus trips made in the novel.

And while the interest in sex was to become much more specific and elaborate as Percy continued to write novels, "The Man on the Train" ends with an observation that somewhat applies to Binx's "desire": "In Harry Stack Sullivan's words, the mark of success in the culture is how much one can do to another's genitals without risking one's self-esteem unduly" (*MB,* 100).

Other literary motifs are the search for the father, which Binx says is important for him, though he deals with it casually. That theme is not discussed in "The Man on the Train" or elsewhere in Percy's essays, but its somewhat mechanical inclusion in the novel seems to fit the theme of return which Percy discusses in that essay, presumably as a synonym for what he also calls repetition. *The Moviegoer* does not mention the motif of return, which, however, *The Last Gentleman* uses specifically to explain Will's trip home to the South. This repetition, ironically, includes the search for his father. While the essays give examples of these techniques of repetition (Thomas Wolfe's work) and rotation (*Huck Finn*), sufficient to indicate that Percy knows what he is talking about, *The Moviegoer* itself awkwardly stops to define and illustrate them by naming movies and then moving on to show its own examples of them.

Now, two matters are pertinent here: the limits of the literary techniques and the use of literature; and the success of Percy's attempt to relieve alienation. For the first matter, Percy makes it clear in the essay that the relief is aesthetic and not existential. Thus, it is temporary and not necessarily permanent; superficial and not ultimate. The ultimate cure of the malady rather than relief of the symptoms would be enduring the search and reaching the goal—finding God. God is the only real answer and the self the only certifier and certified. Thus, religion is necessary. Signs of the cure, though, would likely involve giving up business interests, mere moneymaking, and desire, the wish and the attempt to use another's genitals for whatever purpose but that associated with life. Both of these Binx does, as he begins his vocation.

The other matter, whether Percy successfully illustrates his theory and achieves his intent to relieve alienation, would require testimony from each reader. Binx himself reads *Arabia Deserta*, another tale of a man in a desert wasteland reading beautiful descriptions (*M*, 214). The youthful romantic on the bus reading *The Charterhouse of Parma* about a youthful romantic in nineteenth-century France is not going to know that he is a moviegoer. Would reading *Nausea, The Age of Reason*, or *The Stranger* be preferable somehow? Well, the judges for the National Book Award seemed to think Percy offered either a shock of recognition or a spasm of nostalgia to "every—or nearly every—American" (opposite the title page). But if the nostalgia is associated with movies, Binx's moviegoing is, as noted above, obscure as either a symptom of the malady or a sign of the cure. And the allusions could have been meaningful only for readers approximately Percy's age with a disposition to recognize something Percy or Kierkegaard calls despair. The doctrines are used in the novel, but what they accomplish is unclear.

As for the shock of recognition, the abyss is obvious, but such things as Binx's superciliousness and his logorrhea about Chicago do nothing to help relieve alienation unless complaint, the age-old remedy, helps. He otherwise only encourages development of a clique. *The Moviegoer* does nothing to help with alienation.

Chapter Six
The Last Gentleman

The Last Gentleman is a picaresque, told in the third person, of the adventures and ideas of Williston (Will) Bibb Barrett. Will is like Binx in being the scion of an old Southern family in decline. His mother is never mentioned, and his father committed suicide at some vague time, with a shotgun blast to his chest, leaving Will deaf in one ear from a psychological wound. He attempts to explain the unaccountable event, a death in victory, when he thought his liberal father had defeated the racial bigots. He possibly never understands that his father died to avoid not the bigotry but the immorality of the age.

Whether or not they derive from the trauma of his father's suicide, Will has a good many mental problems. He has periods of amnesia, déjà vus, fugues, racial memories, and atavistic recollections of incidents that may have occurred to one of his ancestors. And his dislocation in space quite complements his temporal disorientation. Will's difficulties, including his search both to know what his father did and for a father substitute take him to the Southwest and finally back to Alabama. *The Last Gentleman* is a comic version of the traditional heroic quest for adventure and accomplishment, and it, too, may be designed to illustrate Percy's theories about relief of alienation.

His concern with American culture leads him to compose a topical subplot that deals with the civil rights movement in the sixties, an effort justified somewhat by the attempt to analyze the complexities of racial difficulties in the South instead of promulgating the simplistic "liberal" view.

The main plot in a novel that, despite its length and complication, is hardly plotted, involves Will with a Southern family whose members present the conflicting points of view that Percy wishes to dramatize and which allows him, among other things, to satirize the family saga. The patriarch, a Mr. Vaught, is the wealthy owner of the world's second largest Chevrolet agency. His wife, whose flashing pince-nez is brighter than her mind, opposes fluoridation of water without a glint of reason and interprets the South's defeat in the Civil War as the result of a Jewish conspiracy. Among the offspring, a dying youth of sixteen called Jamie is primarily intended to allow for the miraculous ending of the novel. Next in age is twenty-one-year-old Kitty, who has never been kissed, a wholesome Bama girl resembling a Georgia peach, whom Will adores as either lady or whore. He cannot tell which until he discovers himself and also discerns the way of the world, neither of which really occurs in the course of the novel. Sex and love are major aspects of Will's problem, and they are the main theme of the novel. Two older children, Sutter and Val, and Sutter's divorced wife Rita, are the main characters in this novel, and are actually more important than Will, who absorbs without much effect all their views.

Here too, as in all the novels, Percy uses a dialectical exchange of points of view. Rita, by no means a pleasant woman, is an artistic humanist, maybe a friend of Sam Yerger and his cosmopolite wife in *The Moviegoer*. She is an important officer in a foundation, and she encourages Indian (Native American) lads to improve themselves by such means as going to Harvard. She is also sexually ambiguous for some reason never clearly related to the logic of the narrative.

Set against her and everything she possibly could stand for, and set against each other as everlasting if friendly antagonists, are Sutter, the oldest child, a doctor who calls himself a pornographer, and Val, who has become a devoted if not devout Roman Catholic with a mission among some deprived blacks. The conflict of ideologies presented in *The Moviegoer* is sharpened. Now Roman Catholicism is forthrightly introduced rather than being merely a weak alternative to the dignified stoicism of an intent Aunt Emily, and the mentally ravaged Sutter is not merely the opinionated Binx but one of the dispossessed. The novel ends with the death of the youngest child, leaving Val on the way to take charge of funeral arrangements, Sutter to wander without cause, and Will to return to Kitty and pursuit of the Little Way in Alabama.

Percy makes numerous revealing comments about the meaning of *The Last Gentleman*, and they encourage the idea that Will is the significant character. In fact, he may be what Mann in *The Magic Mountain* calls "life's delicate child," whose soul is battleground for forces of the rational and the irrational. Percy tells one interviewer,

"This young man, Will Barrett, was both a great deal worse off than Binx and better off. He was worse off because he was sick; he was really sick. . . . He really existed in what Kierkegaard would call the religious mode. . . . The abyss was always yawning at his feet. The book is nothing but a journey. The question, you see, is whether it is better to be a drowning man, or alive and well in East Orange."[1]

To another interviewer, he says, "Barrett, on the other hand, has a passionate pilgrimage that he must follow, and he is looking for a father-figure. His symptoms are ambiguous, however, and he could go in various directions. The ambiguity is deliberate. The reader is free to see him as a sick man among healthy business men or as a sane pilgrim in a mad world."[2] And on another occasion:

I wanted him seen as a patient, an ill man suffering all kinds of difficulties. . . . he was trying to "engineer" his own life, an impossible task. But I think most of the satire here comes from a different design of the book. It is a novel of the return. A young man returns from New York to the South in a bad time—the 1960's—when the racial conflict was at its peak. There were those really wild, extreme reactions, almost paranoid reactions of segregationists to integration. A good deal of it was satire directed to events happening in the South.[3]

But on this satire he makes a serious comment: "I suppose the physical travels of my main character were the physical analogue of his spiritual odyssey. He was on the move geographically and spiritually at the same time. It seemed appropriate for him to be moving. He is *Homo viator*."[4] He is also of course Percy's Huck Finn, and he may be designed to promote the theory mentioned at the end of the last chapter about alienation.

On another occasion, Percy says, "I am not sure what happened to Barrett. He probably went back to the South, married Kitty, and worked in the Chevrolet agency. He never knew what was going on. He kept asking Sutter what to do and Sutter refused to tell him."[5] And Percy adds elsewhere,

He knows that people know something he doesn't know . . . , and in the death scene a baptism takes place, with a very ordinary sort of priest, a mediocre priest. And here again, Barrett has eliminated Christianity. . . . It's not even to be spoken of, taken seriously, or anything else. . . . Well, it ends, unlike *The Moviegoer,* with Barrett missing it, like Kate missed it. He *misses* it! . . . So presumably . . . Barrett, who existed in a religious mode of search, repetition, and going into the desert, which are all in Kierkegaard's religious mode, at the end misses it.[6]

Christendom

In *The Moviegoer,* Binx calls upon Rory Calhoun to hear his plaint about the impossible sexual dichotomy of the Western world, some indefinable position between a pagan creed outworn and the Christian ideal outdated. This "sad post-Christian sex" has driven Sutter to honesty. He is, as a lewd pornographer, "the only sincere American" (*LG,* 292), he says. Others are hypocrites searching for sex as something forbidden, and yet others are unable to find and enjoy. He resolves the dualisms, actually the conflict of humanism, hypocrisy, and purity, by choosing self-exile in which he openly practices what he calls pornography, the nearly indiscriminate sexual cultivation of women that Binx so much desires. He anticipates Tom More in loving all women, though he is far too intense to enjoy anything else.

Thus, Percy's interest in this novel is not merely with Will Barrett's welfare but in attacking Christendom, with its two moral failures, sexual indulgence and enslavement of blacks. And he now clearly intends to write a Catholic novel and not one that is a part of all that he has met. In this design Will, who is charming and more pleasant than Percy's other characters, serves a purpose. Percy is probably experimenting with his own theories about sexual purity. Some years later Percy will have Lancelot specifically say he is not railing about youthful sexual indulgences in college, which appear to have no bearing on the matter of fidelity or marriage. But here in *The Last Gentleman* Percy attempts to present a virile youth who remains sexually pure, in part by physically working off his energy. The question was whether Percy himself wished to promote so thorough a sexual purity as being in any way reasonable or possible for anyone except a man preparing for the priesthood.

This attempt to present fully masculine and sexually clean youth presumably explains the unnecessary references to homosexuality here (though it does not explain their unnecessary appearance elsewhere in Percy's novels). Can he keep a virile youth virginal as he presents aspects of the traditional view of Christian morality? If Will successfully bears this impossible weight, it is only because he is bewildered and thus subject to the author's ironic tone and therefore the reader's ironic perception of his aberrant activities. (Percy is relatively more successful in *The Second Coming,* where Will is too preoccupied to succumb to the entreaties of the forthright Kitty. He can plausibly remain celibate until he falls in love with Allison with whom he is indulgent as they make plans to marry. Intention to marry rather than burn does appear to excuse premarital sexual intercourse, according to Kate's remark to Binx and Tom's to Ellen about marriage plans and honorable intentions.)

To make the moral failure of Christendom poignant, Percy both creates the mentally extravagant Sutter and sets for Will the impossible question whether women are ladies or whores and whether love is "a sweetnesse or a wantonnesse" (*LG,* 110). Love is the main theme of this novel as it is of all Percy's works, including *The Moviegoer.* Sutter finally at the end of the action blurts out in exasperation that he thinks all of Will's questions and questing really meant he wanted to be told whether or not to fornicate, indulge in sex as an unmarried man in a Christian culture. And that is precisely Will's question, though he asks it of the universe and not of Sutter alone. Sutter is surrogate for the universe. And no wonder Will is obsessed. His father killed himself over a closely related matter of personal morality. In a wider sense, Will's question is, What does it take to be a man? But before Sutter's statement of the problem, never resolved in this novel, in part because Sutter has no idea what to reply, other investigations of love appear.

Love

First is the question of what love is. Will at once knows he loves Kitty when he sees her in Central Park, but he has no idea what action ought to follow from that conviction. Much of what occurs in the book and all of what occurs between Will and Kitty is a confused attempt to decide what actions and activity such an attraction involves in the ambivalent moral situation the culture provides. Finding themselves as young people literally means finding proper sexual activity. Kitty also has no idea what to do, though boldness may be incipient in her. Is she to be a lady at the dining table or a whore in the bedroom showing sexual desire as a man does?

Val offers a stern Christian love that makes her devote herself to nearly mute black children, while Sutter argues for the dark and

Dionysian (as well as the destructive) forces of sex. Rita is androgynous and sterile, and the most she can do is study Erich Fromm's *Art of Loving,* in some attempt to get her experience from a book. Myra Thigpen, Mr. Vaught's daughter from an earlier marriage, has a son who rattles his Thunderbird keys, pats himself potently, and mentions poontang a lot. Besides Rita's determined, vague, humanistic love for the unfortunate and Son Thigpen's reduction of life to combining Christian Hellenism's high ideals and poontang, is the elder Vaught's bemused paternal affection that leads him to give each of his offspring a check for a hundred thousand dollars on his twenty-first birthday if he has neither drunk alcohol nor smoked cigarettes. He says nothing of sex, having of course no idea what to say, much as he may know about Sutter's activities.

The seriousness of the topic of love appears particularly in references to two literary works, the latest novel by Mort Prince, a summary statement of Mort's philosophy entitled *Love,* and a play by the nameless black playwright whom Will meets in Ithaca. Mort Prince appears early in the narrative: *"Love* was about orgasms, good and bad, some forty-six. But it ended, as Forney had said, on a religious note. 'And so I humbly ask of life,' said the hero to his last partner with whose assistance he had managed to coincide with his best expectations, 'that it grant us the only salvation, that of one human being discovering himself through another and through the miracle of love' " (*LG,* 138). While something of this kind of interaction appears to be encouraged in some of Percy's essays and while a version of it is dramatized in *The Second Coming,* the obvious difficulty here is that the situation is purely humanistic, and nothing is said in all this string of adulteries about divine love and its relationship to salvation. Ironically, among all the other ironies in this passage, Will receives the volume *Love* from Forney Aiken's daughter in a nightie, who has come to give him whatever she has that he might want, being a good old girl with nothing to lose and maybe something to give. And what may be the ultimate for Percy's sense of irony: Mort's character's wish is more or less in the form of a prayer about salvation.

The black dramatist writes

about an artist who has gone stale, lost his creative powers, until he musters the courage to face the truth within himself, which is his love for his wife's younger brother. He puts a merciful end to the joyless uncreative marriage in favor of a more meaningful relationship with his friend. The last scene shows the lovers standing in a window of the artist's Left Bank apartment looking up at the gleaming towers of Sacre-Coeur. "There has been a loss of the holy in the world," said the youth. "Yes, we must recover it," replies the artist. "It has fallen to us to recover the holy." "It has been a long time since I was at Mass," says the youth, looking at the church. "Let's have our own Mass," replies the artist as softly as Pelleas and, stretching forth a shy hand, touches the youth's golden hair (*LG*, 322).

A passage of this sort, with and without its ironies, among them making a religion of sex, presents approximately the antithesis of what Percy encourages.

But Percy's strongest comment may be the understatement about another of Mort Prince's novels in which a writer "enters into a sexual relationship with a housewife next door, not as a conventional adultery, for he was not even attracted to her, but rather as the exercise of that last and inalienable possession of the individual in a sick society, freedom" (*LG*, 140). Percy of course would consider this kind of writing as well as the incident it records as the real sign of the sickness of the society. This misuse of self and another in the exercise of something called freedom is nothing more than the "right" to sin capriciously. Ironically, the idea here is somehow akin to Sutter's—that sex is the only way of returning from the realm of transcendence.

The theme of love, human and divine, deals eventually with Will's conviction that he loves Kitty as a wife and with the epiphany of divine love at Jamie's death. God's love is all that sexual pleasure cannot provide, all that the organism cannot experience by itself.

Sutter's Casebook

But Sutter is desperate in his love affairs. He maintains a doctrine recognized in the church that sex is one of the ways of moving from the transcendent back to the immanent. Sex might keep him sane by keeping him at least to some extent an inhabitant of the earth. Binx before him had a great ravening desire, if his occasional comments are meaningful regarding the theme of sex, in view of what Percy does in all the later novels. And Tom is consumed with passion in the next novel. Sutter is either practicing a theory or has developed a theory derived from his inclination and practice. He claims, that is, that sexual indulgence is necessary for intellectuals in a highly technological society where they so rarely have to endure ordeals associated with daily living and are therefore free to devise and attempt to realize any generalization or abstraction. *Love in the Ruins* clarifies this matter somewhat. There Percy dramatizes the situation as a threat of annihilation because of ideological conflicts that consume the mind and therefore engage the body. But Percy's favorite example of the ridiculous abstraction is the brotherhood of man and the dignity of the individual, meaningless phrases associated with scientific humanism, in the name of which any atrocity may be committed. Sex, then, quite simply reminds people that they are human beings living in the world and not properly originators and developers of grand plans for the world's salvation. The implication, which however Sutter does not admit, is that God has developed the plan for salvation. Sutter maintains that between religion and science, Christendom and heathenism, the soul is so distrait that only the body's indulgence in sex avails for experiencing the real world. Alienation is such that only sex offers pleasure in the world. Sutter doubts that "purity and life can only come from eating the body and drinking the blood of Christ" (*LG, 282*).

The problem is what Percy finally makes clear in *Love in the Ruins* and what he there calls angelism-bestialism. Man, he says there, is sundered from himself. The idea is that the warfare between science and religion that has been raging since the Renaissance was lost to science or scientific humanism. Man has so much neglected the divine in favoring the human that he has in effect created a new abstraction and a new transcendental realm—a world of the human mind that abstracts him from the world by forcing him to deal in types and cases and laws and generalities without ever dealing with the individual things in the physical world. The world itself, made for his pleasure, has lost its value, though he cannot really escape it; and when he tries to live in it, he no longer has any familiarity with it or its ways. He cannot really operate at the transcendental realm, and his achievements and aspirations mean he is homeless in the immanent realm. Thus, he is more homeless and alienated than he ever was. Sex is the sign of his persistent humanity, but once he has indulged in sex or even merely relieved the physical urge, he has nothing whatever left to do. The physical has forced him to acknowledge being human, but none of the rest of him is.

Lost between these two realms he now has no place. The result is alienation from both worlds.

Sutter is also interested in two abstractions—the brotherhood of man and the dignity of the individual—and in the Christendom that has developed these ideas as it gradually moved away from Christianity. He begins his generalization though not his notebooks with a statement about American culture. "Main Street, U. S. A. = a million-dollar segregated church on one corner, a drugstore with dirty magazines on the other, a lewd movie on the third, and on the fourth a B-girl bar with condom dispensers in the gents' room. Delay-your-climax cream" (*LG*, 292). Christendom is filled with sex and slavery. Segregation, with all its ramifications of inhumanity and injustice, a wealthy "church home" for Christian middle-class businessmen and professional groups, and three avenues to sex; this is Christendom. Purity shows here only in the fact of contraceptives, devices to prevent disease, and even the touch of love.

Sutter, trained as psychiatrist and once physician to the mind, has become not physician of the body but student of dead tissue, and as a pathologist he studies corpses. His casebook is a book of the dead and guide for the perplexed. The first case deals with a conventioneer (an optician who has among other things looked at a pornographic film, a naked woman and nothing else), who possibly had a heart attack while indulging in sex. The second case is a black girl of thirteen killed in racial violence when a church was bombed. The third is a case of suicide. The victim of self-inflicted violence is a man of twenty-five, "well-dev. but under-nour." (*LG*, 344), a technician in a missile development, the latest scientific accomplishment, an example of the well-educated scientist too abstracted, by Percy's theories, to appreciate life in the physical world. Thus, the casebook has three cases of death by violence, one involving sex directly, one involving conflict between races, and one self-inflicted in despair at being unable to exist as divided man.

Into this situation Percy introduces the alternative of Christianity, the old beliefs, to help with all the problems: segregation, the failure of the brotherhood of man; sex, the substitution of the human for the divine, and alienation, simple loss of the creature, as Percy labels it in one of his essays. Here, then, he uses the notebook for the purpose he mentions in an interview, to present the conflicting views, the dialectic between Christianity and unbelief. It is from one point of view the old argument between faith and reason.

Val presumably urges Sutter to "stop fornicating" (*LG,* 373). Literally, that is, she urges him to stop committing a sin in having sexual intercourse outside of marriage. She wants his morals cleaned up. Sutter's response is a discussion of theology. He concedes for the argument at least: "I can understand what you did in the beginning. You opted for the Scandalous Thing, the Wrinkle in Time, the Jew-Christ-Church business, God's alleged intervention in history" (*LG,* 307). Sutter can appreciate this purity of belief in the unbelievable. But he accuses Val of gradually accepting all the impurities that make up Christendom. He names them: "you began to speak of the glories of science, the beauty of art, and the dear lovely world around us! Worst of all, you even embraced . . . the Southern businessman!" (*LG,* 308).

Roman Catholics, like other religious groups, have their beliefs, whatever the problems and doubts. But Sutter has another problem aside from the immoralities and compromises. He says, "I could never accept the propositions (1) that my salvation comes from the Jews, (2) that my salvation depends upon hearing news rather than figuring it out, (3) that I must spend eternity with Southern Baptists" (*LG,* 307). Why, that is, were the Jews chosen to bring Christianity to the world dominated by the foreign culture of Greece and Rome? Why does eternal life depend on an event that is apparently fleeting and random rather than one engendered in the logical essence of being itself? And why can he not figure it out instead of having someone with lesser intellect come and announce it as having authority? And how can narrow-minded bigots and hypocrites also have eternal life when they obviously worship some divinity unknown to the Jesus of history or even the Jews but are also called Christian?

Sutter's argument is of course inconclusive, while Val's are the conclusive arguments of the Christian church. What Sutter does is show their shortcomings for him as one who thinks in what is usually called the rational manner. No purpose would be served if Val were there to reiterate. Sutter, then, shows why he rejects the Christian position, and since he no longer is much interested in indulging his desire for sex, he has about decided to kill himself. Suicide is what is left when sex fails to keep body and soul together. But this matter too is inconclusive, technically. That is, the narrative does not tell of Sutter's violence upon himself. Rather, in fact, despite the conclusions and the inconclusiveness, he may by the end of the action have given up the idea of suicide. He does not change his rationale; he merely does not intend to commit suicide. He may never have intended to do so. His position seems as much like a pose as does that of Binx.

Search for Father and Morality

Meanwhile, Will, courtier and picaro, in this respect anticipating the knight Lancelot, attempts to force Sutter to commit himself about something. Will's search for his father, a subplot that seems designed for suspense, is more integral to the situation here than Binx's search for his father was. Will only gradually makes out what happened in that incident when his father spoke once more of the immorality of the whites and walked off to kill himself. His father's concern makes sense when the theme of fornication is recognized as being so important to the action. The questions for Will's father as for Will himself and for Sutter is sexual morality in Christendom. Sutter has, of course, been the father substitute throughout until Will finds himself temporarily—or thinks he has done so. Actually, one serious conflict in this novel is between Will's father, who concerns himself with morality, and Sutter, who justifies what he calls pornography. This conflict is enhanced both in Will's use of Sutter as father substitute and in his association of the gun and attempted suicide with both characters.

Sutter's substitution as Will's father appears also in a vague outburst in the casebook. Like Val, Sutter says to her, "I turned my back on the bastards and went into the desert. . . . They are going to remake the world and go into space and they couldn't care less whether you and God approve. . . . At least have the courage of your revolt" (LG, 308–9). Soon after he reads this passage, Will goes to the old homeplace in the evening and recalls at last the entire episode of his father's suicide and the motivation, which appears to be not sexual alone but gentlemanly—not desire alone but honor, too. Both points of view, though, protest the trends of the age and criticize the culture: "Once they were the fornicators and the bribers and the takers of bribes and we were not and that was why they hated us. Now we are like them . . ." (LG, 330). Will adds to himself, "It wasn't even his fault because that was the way he was and the way the times were, and there was no other place a man could look" (*LG,* 332).

Though Will attempts to understand instead of blaming his father, Will's father deceived him. Leaving Will on the sidewalk with the impression he would soon return, he went to the attic, deserting Will, to kill himself. Sutter, too, is deserting Will after promising help if he comes asking for it. But what finally helps Will to mature, as much as he does mature in the action, is his acknowledgment of the truth in Sutter's remark: " 'Barrett, since when is failure, my failure, a badge of wisdom?' . . . Suddenly he did see Sutter for the first time as the dismalest failure" (*LG,* 381). Will has substituted Sutter as simply an authority figure, one who, in Percy's terms, states the case, a genius whom Will mistakes for an apostle, a father. This view sends Will off to Santa Fé for answers—on a search for someone to tell him about women and life. So while his question is whether or not to fornicate, he is really asking about the whole way of the world. Is the world made with a possibility that morality has some meaning, or is it made without any discernible meaning?

The shot that Sutter fires after Val, his antagonist, leaves the apartment echoes the shot that Will's father used to kill himself. When they meet Will first asks for psychiatric (physical, professional) help with his nervous disorder. But then almost immediately he asks for everything: "I'm not asking you to practice. I only want to know what you know" (*LG,* 218). Thereafter, he has trouble remembering what he would like to know and in finding the question he would like to have answered. Sutter asks him, in the catechism about his father, while Will, sensing Sutter's boredom, wishes Sutter would tell him how the story came out. A few days later, a section deals with Will's dream of his father and of a shot that sends him to the Vaught attic. And as he left "the youth called out to him. 'Wait' " (*LG,* 331), as he calls to Sutter who does wait, whose "Edsel paused, sighed, and stopped" (*LG,* 409). Sutter is not going to commit suicide. A Roman Catholic novelist is not going to portray a suicide, especially when there is a chance that a miracle has been performed at Jamie's bedside.

Divine Love

One of Percy's finest accomplishments is the remarkable account of Jamie's death. The passage is the more impressive because it at first seems abrupt and unmotivated in a rambling novel concerned with Will's vagaries and all the ills of Christendom. Actually, however, the scene is designed to end a Christian novel and to intensify if not resolve the dialogue between Sutter and the Christian religion, within which Will (and now Jamie) is life's delicate child. And what is superbly poignant is that Jamie, Sutter's brother, is Sutter's last case of death.

The Sutter who abstractedly wanders in search of the concrete and of a way to bond soul and body against Christendom has in Jamie's death the ultimate interplay between transcendent and immanent. While the priest is in process of baptizing Jamie for his soul's welfare, the body intrudes persistently with sublime mortality: "After a moment there arose to the engineer's nostrils first an intimation, like a new presence in the room, a somebody, then a foulness beyond the compass of smell. This could only be the dread ultimate rot of the molecules themselves, an abject surrender. It was the body's disgorgement of its most secret shame. Doesn't this ruin everything, wondered the engineer . . ." (*LG*, 401).

One of the best aspects of the scene, no matter what the views about religion, is the creed that Father Boomer eloquently and simply states as a question to the dying youth.

"Do you accept the truth that God exists and that He made you and loves you and that He made the world so that you might enjoy its beauty and that He himself is your final end and happiness, that He loved you so much that He sent His only Son to die for you and to found His Holy Catholic Church so that you may enter heaven and there see God face to face and be happy with Him forever?" (*LG*, 403).

It is sublime rote, and it is addressed to every reader. Jamie appears gradually to become persuaded in this passage, too abruptly for any dramatic motive except divine intervention, but Percy probably wishes to suggest the idea that the authority of the messenger leads to belief in the one simple truth. The priest is an unpretentious man familiar with orthodox Roman church practice and above all with dying. He has seen everything without losing faith. And he too represents Percy's concept borrowed from Kierkegaard of the distinction between the genius and the apostle. When Jamie asks why he should believe, Father Boomer says, " 'It is true because God Himself revealed it as the truth!' " Jamie asks what makes him sure. "The priest sighed. 'If it were not true,' he said to Jamie, 'then I would not be here. That is why I am here, to tell you.' " (*LG*, 404). It is beautiful whether anyone believes it or not. Priests are there talking about salvation because Primal Being called God promises something called salvation to those who realize they are lost souls. The confrontation forces both Will and Sutter to define themselves at least temporarily. Will has been in process of discovery since the conversation with Sutter astonished him. And with the "last of the dudes," as Jamie lay dying, Sutter may resolve his romantic conflict in a measure of common sense. Presumably "The Edsel waited" so Sutter could listen to Will—even if it is only another question. That question may deal with whether Jamie died satisfactorily. Death in Christendom is the problem for Sutter. Why is Jamie dying? is the question for him. His encounter with religion changes him, however. Jamie's death gave him life. And Will's question may be whether death is another way of moving from transcendental to immanent—or the only way from immanent to transcendental.

Sending Will back to marry Kitty seems either incomprehensible or impossible, since Percy lets the reader expect something of Will's indeterminate potential. Something should come of this young man and his search. But, as Percy says, though Will is a shrewd youth, "he misses it." He failed to see the epiphany, though he has spent the entire period of the book seeing with the artificial aid, and from the quiet of his burrow through the bullet hole in Sutter's apartment wall. He has watched and waited and seen nothing. But then, too, Binx thought something might be said for living the Little Way in Gentilly. And even when he recovered from that pose and married, he settled in one of Nell Lovell's ready made houses, in school, living quietly with Kate, promising to make something like his little contribution. Closing sales is important to a business. Kitty can take care of Will better than Kate can do for Binx. Only Sutter (and sometimes the ironic narrator) has doubts about Captain Mickle's house. Will and Kitty may even find their church home. He is a good wanderer, but he may not be quite ready for a full, earnest search for being. His return to faithful married life with Kitty is precisely what Percy thinks proper for a young man.

Chapter Seven
Love in the Ruins

Christendom

Love is the theme, and the ruins are the unromantic wasteland of Christendom, particularly of course the United States, with its dream of the brotherhood of man serving God. Tom More, descendent of the Renaissance Christian who wrote about utopia, which America wanted to be, is at the intersection of the interstate waiting and watching. He expects nothing much, except the worst, an explosion that will turn all the numerous political antagonists to violence and mutual obliteration. He thinks that at last, without God's urging, or perhaps with it, man is going to destroy his technological utopia. The main action occurs during the first four days of July in some indeterminate but possibly near future (maybe 1983), these "dread latter days" (*LR,* 3), having begun when a member of an ill-organized group of Bantus led by a rabid Ph.D. from Ann Arbor began their revolution by shooting at Tom's house. Blacks are seeking their own independence day. Signs of decay of the white man's culture are everywhere, vines even in the bar of the segregated country club, and appearances indicate that on this July Fourth, when the country celebrates its birthday as the new Eden and the new republic, destruction is imminent.

Rather a parallel plot than a subplot, this threat continues throughout the novel, providing violence in association with a plot dealing with sex. Tom actually is in Kierkegaard's musical-erotic state, having become a "bad Catholic" by losing his religion when his daughter Samantha died and his wife ran off with a "heathen Englishman," a creature not unlike one of Percy's Swedes or Californians in his Godlessness. Tom fell so low as to attempt suicide after an erotic encounter with a musician, Lola, one of three girls he wishes to save from holocaust, and a musical encounter with an ancient Perry Como, both on Christmas eve, when a good Catholic would have been at midnight Mass, waiting and watching for God's presence. This theme of sex and love dominates the book not only because of Tom's diverse activities but also because it is one of the major activities of this enclave composed of Paradise Estates, Fedville, and the town.

Yet a third narrative tells of Tom's development of a mechanism, a sensitive product of combined science and technology, the ultimate outcome of behaviorism and the "scientific" study of being, that will diagnose and perhaps eventually cure the malady of Western man, driven body from soul ever since Descartes finished what the Renaissance started. Here the problem is the dichotomy of angelism and bestialism, one of Percy's terms for the sundered self that is Western man.

Thus, Tom is mainly a mad scientist, who is a bad Catholic in part because of his extremely humanistic pride as the inventor of a machine to cure all ills of the spirit, a task that God has assigned himself. The identification with Faust is obvious and deliberate. In aiming so high, however, Tom attempts to replace God as physician-savior to the self. And this pride, symbolized by his hope to win acclaim through receiving the Nobel prize, leads to his rebellion against God—precisely what humanistic Western man does. Tom's dream is to "weld the broken self whole!" (*LR, 36*).

Percy's comments emphasize this point: "Dr. More was a diagnostician. He knew something was wrong but he fell victim to pride, was seduced by the devil. Immelmann was the devil, of course, who showed Dr. More how to cure. It worked for a while. . . . The big mistake was in him, that he could believe he could treat a spiritual disease with a scientific device however sophisticated."[1] Percy observes in the same interview: "The view of Pascal and some others who were interested in the human condition was that there is something wrong with mankind. So it is always undecided in my novels. This is the main question of the novels. Here is a hero who is afflicted, shows malaise, dislocation, and he is surrounded by apparently happy and sane people, particularly Dr. More, who lives in Paradise Estates. So who is crazy, the people apparently happy or those radically dislocated characters?"[2]

Angelism and Bestialism

These words are new terminology for the kind of dichotomy Sutter in *The Last Gentleman* calls respectively transcendence and immanence. The danger for Western man is that he might become "totally abstracted from himself, totally alienated from the concrete world, and in such a state of angelism that he will fall prey to the first abstract notion proposed to him and will kill anybody who gets in his way, torture, execute, wipe out entire populations, all with the best possible motives and the best possible intentions, in fact in the name of peace and freedom, etcetera" (LG, 328). Extreme individuality is one problem, antinomianism in religion, a combination of pride, ignorance and ego mistakenly convinced of its intuitive relationship with deity. And unfortunately a man can have angelism and bestialism simultaneously, be both "extremely abstracted and inordinately lustful" (LG, 27). Will, Sutter, and even Binx, despite his interest in the concrete, all suffer from this malady. Any imbalance may lead to extremes. The worst deals with love: "It seems the murderers who have terrorized this district for the past ten years turned out to be neither black guerrillas nor white Knotheads but rather a love community in the swamp. The leader is quoted as saying his family believes in love, the environment, and freedom of the individual" (LR, 387).

Tom's own problem is abstraction and inordinate lust. He has been awhirl among theories as student of the head, encephalographer. The creed that he states early in the novel shows his difficulty: "I believe in God and the whole business but I love women best, music and science next, whiskey next, God fourth, and my fellowman hardly at all" (LR, 6). Such remarks immediately introduce the main theme, the other word in the title—love in the Western world and sex in Christendom. All this is emphasized later when Art Immelmann, the devil's avatar, advises Tom to go to his women: "Love them! Work on your invention. Stimulate your musical-erotic! Develop your genius. . . . Work! Love! Music! That's what makes a man happy" (LR, 364). As Art says elsewhere, the devil's job is to encourage people to cultivate their shortcomings and submit to their indispositions.

Here too Percy uses Kierkegaard's distinction between the genius and the apostle. While Tom is well aware of the tension between body and soul, he is also a doctor, a scientist, a psychiatrist whose work is the attempt to join body and soul. Everyone recognizes his genius, the potential for his research (like Binx's), his diagnostic abilities (like Sutter's), and his great potential (like Will's). He calls himself a genius, and others would think him "some kind of genius"

(*LR*, 11). Immelmann later tells him to develop his genius. But his message has no authority. People either do not listen or else think he is crazy. Ultimately, he has no authority, thus has nothing to offer. He is just another one of those nay-sayers who threaten destruction. Besides, a scientist with a machine cannot help Western man. Only the proctologists and psychoanalysts, one treating the body for large bowel complaint (because it is stuffed with refuse) and the other ministering to the head full of nonsense, can be of temporary help.

Dystopias

Love in the Ruins is a dystopia designed to reveal the deficiencies in humanistic attempts at building utopias and possibly even those with God at the center. It really deals with another moral wasteland, more specifically outlined here than in either preceding novel. Both the religious and the political experiments have failed in America. Christianity has become repressive Christendom, needing reform more than did the church of the Middle Ages, and distinctions are still made between rich and poor, privileged and bonded, and especially between white and black.

But alternatives without religion are discarded. Paradise Estates, with its fences and patrolling guards, is for upper-middle-class professionals (proctologists and psychiatrists) who treat body and soul, or one another, and fail. Fedville is a complex for the care and feeding of scientists, a pretentious enclave funded by taxes. It includes Love Clinic which proposes to resolve the whole matter of sex and love by reducing intangible emotions to the antic behavior of lustful attractiveness. Gerry Rehab is devoted to the aged, who, when the time comes, go off to easeful death and lose the dignity of living even that experience, so important to existentialists because it individualizes.

Within this framework is the swamp, itself filled with dystopias. Some, like the revolutionary Bantu, are banished there; some use the place for sanctuary. But the outcasts deserve little consideration. Uru, finally, wants to "Take what we need, destroy what we don't, and live in peace and brotherhood" (*LR*, 372). To this ethic Tom replies, "You got to get to where we are or where you think we are and I'm not even sure you can do that" (*LR*, 373), one of Percy's reiterated observations about blacks. This foiled attempt leads to the quiet monetary revolution that gives Paradise Estates to the Bantus, establishing a new order with the old prejudices now directed at the whites, showing the deplorable weaknesses in the materialistic ideal of freedom.

Each of the factions in the Catholic church represents utopian ideals, as divisions in religion always have claimed to do, and they are too dreary to discuss in any detail except to note that M. Schleifkopf (Knothead) follows the old tradition in the South of justifying slavery on the basis of Christ's having ignored the subject.

Chuck's outline of his hopes best represents the views of the supposedly idealistic youth of the sixties (when the novel was written). When he appears as one of the tempters in the events of the last short period of the action, he says: "We'll start a new life in a new world. . . . then we'll live on Bayou Pontchatalawa, which means peace, and love one another and watch the seasons come and smoke a little cannab in the evenings . . . and live on catfish and Indian maize and wild grape and raise good sweet innocent children" (LR, 367–68). If Percy is an orthodox Catholic, he would consider this nonsense invincible ignorance and an impossible parody of the idea of wanting, watching, and waiting. These youths will have nothing to do with either God or man, and this ideal is merely another kind of rejection of life. Children are conceived in sin, according to the church; and while they might grow in grace, they never would be innocent.

The Uses of Love

Almost every aspect of love is entertained in the novel. Tom loves three girls and thereby three kinds of women, besides his former wife Doris and his daughter Samantha. His former wife was a romantic who in middle age tended to think of love as a spiritual thing. She was an intellectual woman of pretentions, abstracted from herself somewhat as Margot is in *Lancelot*. Her kind of love seems to mean nothing to Percy's men. Samantha represents Christian love. Moira, one of the women, who thinks Montovani is classical music, and who dwells intellectually on salesmen and flappers, represents man's fate, his inherent commitment to sex. She may be somewhat below the scale of Binx's Lindas and Sharons. Lola, the cellist, incarnates and combines the musical and the erotic, possibly as an avatar of Lilith, the dark lady of the unconscious.

She has a great lust for life and horse. The third is Ellen, whom Tom finally marries, a good Presbyterian who settles for no nonsense in either religion or sex. She is designed to have children, not indulge in the flesh for the pleasure of it.

But before this action is resolved, Tom speaks much more of love. One main approach is satirical. In the clinic—"In 'Love,' as it is called, volunteers perform sexual acts singly, in couples, and in groups, beyond viewing mirrors in order that man might learn more about the human sexual response" (*LR,* 14). Percy started this satire on behaviorism and the idea of a scientific study of love, the subjective, individual, and unaccountable in human experience, in *The Moviegoer* where he lets Binx fantasize about the private antics of an elderly couple resembling Masters and Johnson, superficially. Love in Christendom has so degenerated that a priest has left the church to watch the vaginal console, where Helga, the German scientist, and others study all the physiological aspects of romance. These behaviorists suggest that man is nothing more than an organism and that he does not even have the capacity for angelism, bad as that condition may be. The priest has exchanged divine love for voyeurism.

Another example of love is that of Chuck and Janet, the hippies living in the swamp. He is a bright Anglo-Saxon and she Jewish, who have gone natural and produced a love child. Chuck talks of the good life, and, among other things, says, to the wise old Tom, with all the ingenuousness of a great pastoral naïf, "There's nothing wrong with sex, Doc" (*LR,* 51).

While Tom revels in guiltless sex (more relaxed than Sutter and unburdened with a philosophy), he often recalls the time when he was a better Catholic, inspired in some measure by his love for his ugly daughter Samantha, a figure of Beatrice in this divine comedy and possibly something like the pearl of great price. She "turned out to be chubby, fair, acned, and pious, the sort who likes to hang around after school and beat Sister's erasers" (*LR,* 12), to the disappointment of her romantic mother. He cries when he recalls her death, as he does three or four times during these four days. "The best of times," he says, "were after mass on summer evenings when Samantha and I would walk home in the violet dusk, we having received Communion and I rejoicing afterwards, caring nought for my fellow Catholics but only for myself and Samantha and Christ swallowed, remembering what he promised me for eating him, that .

I would have life in me, and I did, feeling so good that I'd sing and cut the fool all the way home like King David before the Ark" (*LR*, 12–13).

But while this memory may keep Tom dreaming of divine love, he but gradually arrives at the realization of his love for Ellen and at a philosophy of love. He first hints at his realization when at some time while they are in the motel he thinks, "How shabby Ellen makes it all seem!" (*LR*, 336). While the situation is all parody, of the eternal feminine theme and the Gretchen episode in *Faust*, Ellen shows her love in her willingness to sacrifice her "treasure trove" to Art Immelmann in order to save Tom. And Tom says she is right to follow her aunt's advice and keep her virginity for her husband.

But despite his love for all women, Tom makes a distinction near the end of the action as he perceives that Ellen is his one true woman. He will marry, he says, both Lola and Moira instead of being forced to choose.

> "It's a question of honor."
> "Honor?"
> "I don't believe a man should trifle with a girl."
> "Well yes, but—!"
> "However, if a man's intentions are honorable—" (*LR*, 344)

When Ellen suggests he contemplates an illegal polygamy, he considers that " 'These are peculiar times' " and adds, " 'Abraham had several wives.' " Some dream of another world may complicate this situation. But this matter of intent in this theme of love and honor seems to make all the difference to Percy. Tom was worried that he feels no guilt for what he calls his fornication with Lola on Christmas Eve before he attempted suicide. In an exchange with Max, who attempts to diagnose the malady, he says lovemaking is sinful " 'Only between persons not married to each other' " (*LR*, 116). A collection of such observations, beginning with Kate's insistence that Binx should have told Aunt Emily that they were planning to marry, makes legalization of normal sex through marriage appear to be the highest ideal in Percy's moral code. These unassuming lines about intent are statements as to what these edifying discourses of Percy's are all about.

Salvation

Don Giovanni (Juan), the careless lover, goes to eternal damnation; Faust, the struggler, and Dante the faithful are saved. Paradise is lost through a woman and sex and saved through the eternal feminine: Beatrice calls Dante through a series of steps to Lucia and the Virgin then to Christ. Gretchen, whom Faust has seduced, helps to save him at the end of his long life of striving. Paradise is lost through Doris, Tom's first wife, who falls for the English con man with his interest in Hindus and boys, and regained through Ellen. Tom returns to the garden to work. He gradually moves upward in his loves like a Platonic man, through refinement to divine knowledge—as he goes from Doris the romantic through Moira, man's fate, through Lola, the hissing temptress, to Ellen and God.

Through a series of easily overlooked comments and actions, Percy gradually returns Tom to the church and something resembling its ideals. When he goes to church with his mother, he discovers he cannot endure the theology of slavery and Property Rights Sunday, so he goes off to his old church where Father Smith, anonymous like Percy's other priestly divine messengers but recovered from the madness he suffered in knowing the message was jammed, holds service for a few in the old slave quarters. Among them, the "leftovers," Tom thinks, is

A love couple from the swamp, dressed in rags and seashells, who, having lived a free life, chanted mantras, smoked Choctaw cannab, lain together dreaming in the gold-green world, conceived and borne children, dwelled in a salt mine—chanced one day upon a Confederate Bible, read it as if it had never been read before, the wildest unlikeliest doctrine imaginable, believed it, decided to be married and baptize their children. (*LR*, 187–88)

Earlier, Tom diagnoses his problem and prays:

Dear God, I can see it now, why can't I see it other times, that it is you I love in the beauty of the world and in all the lovely girls and dear good friends, and it is pilgrims we are, wayfarers on a journey, and not pigs, nor angels. (*LR*, 109)

When he finally goes to confession, Father Smith says clearly, without the message being jammed, "You are also a husband and father and it is your duty to love and cherish your family" (*LR*, 398).

Percy offers a helpful comment about *Love in the Ruins*. Using
Tom's interest in science gave him, he says, a chance "to say what
I wanted to say about contemporary issues. About polarization: there
are half a dozen of them: black-white, North-South, young-old,
affluent-poor, etc." He continues:

And do not forget that at the end of *Love in the Ruins* there is a suggestion
of a new community, new reconciliation. It has been called a pessimistic
novel but I do not think it is. A renewed community is suggested. The
suggestion is in the last scene which takes place in a midnight mass between
a Christmas Saturday and Sunday. The Catholics, the Jews come to the
midnight mass, also the unbelievers in the same community. The great
difference between Dr. More and the other heroes is that Dr. More has
no philosophical problems. He knows what he believes.

And in his next reply to the interviewer's question, he says it is a
religious reconciliation and adds, "This was meant for Southerners
in particular and for Americans in general."[3]
    That is, the dualisms are synthesized, more or less, and the main
character is admittedly religious. He knows he believes. He is no
longer a bad Catholic, one only in name, as he called himself at the
beginning of the story. He now practices. He has enjoyed two
sacraments, marriage and mass. Percy's suggestion of a new community may be overdone, but the novel does at least show Tom
back in the church. *That* reunion in fact is the beauty of the novel.
    What is left of Tom's ordeal in the narrative proper of July First
through Fourth and in the forces of the past leading to these few
days is the kind of creed that the athletic, unassuming and unpriestly
apostle Father Smith—a nonentity as his name indicates—delivers
extemporaneously in the epilogue: "Meanwhile, forgive me but there
are other things we must think about: like doing our jobs, you
being a better doctor, I being a better priest, showing a bit of
ordinary kindness to people, particularly our own families . . .
doing what we can for our poor unhappy country . . ." (*LR*, 399).
Even the possibility of the old religious caritas may appear in the
little group of Catholics who meet for Mass in the epilogue, and
these virtues are age-old and ordinary. The tone here differs somewhat from that of Binx with his "good and selfish reasons." The
content may also be a little different. The concern is broader, and
the outlook involves more people.

The epilogue also offers a kind of resolution to Tom's personal problem and his pride in his scientific achievement. He has talked of watching and waiting, not merely at the intersection of the interstate. The vocation of the wayfarer is "serene skimming watchfulness" (*LR*, 105). In the epilogue, he is "Waiting and listening and looking at my boots" (*LR*, 381). Finally, after all the pyrotechnics of the narrative and the journey, he says, "the world is broken, sundered, busted down the middle, self ripped from self and man pasted back together as a mythical monster, half angel, half beast, but no man. Even now I can diagnose and shall one day cure: cure the new plague. . . . Some day a man will walk into my office as ghost or beast or ghost-beast and walk out as a man, which is to say sovereign wanderer, lordly exile, worker and waiter and watcher" (*LR*, 382–83). The resolution lies in part in making Tom's work a part of some divine plan.

But when all else is done, at the very end of *Love in the Ruins* is the jewel of the book and maybe of Percy's work. Tom has a new family. He is inferior to the new order of black professionals. He lives in the slave quarters and has not always enough to eat. He has just managed to pay for Ellen's Christmas present. And he has been to confession for the first time since he went with Samantha. Everything is in its place. All's right with the world. He says, "I'm dancing around to keep warm, hands in pockets. It is Christmas Day and the Lord is here, a holy night and surely that is all one needs" (*LR*, 402). This is a divine comedy, this final antic dance of the holy fool. On another Christmas Day he attempted suicide. Now he is for the dear life "cutting the fool like David before the ark" (*LR*, 402). And then, quite anticipating *The Second Coming*, though that novel properly reverses the order of loves, in the love of God he goes off to bed with Ellen for joyous human love.

Chapter Eight
Lancelot

The narrative is in the first person, a kind of confession of activities to a doctor of both body and soul, a physician-priest, named Percival, among other names, with whom the narrator grew up near New Orleans. Their families were Anglo-Saxon Episcopal, though Percival has converted and become a Roman Catholic priest. The author is explicit about their origins because they are examples of what has happened to the best people in the moral wasteland of Christendom. As the "we" whom Will Barrett's father scorns in *The Last Gentleman*, fornicators and takers of bribes, they are the ironic equivalents of the Knights of the Round Table in King Arthur's court, whose Christian world was destroyed in the interaction of sexual and theological, earthly and divine love, wherein the main figure, Lancelot, while epitomizing the cultural ideals also effectively destroyed the utopia because he committed adultery with the queen, one of the rulers of the land. Lancelot and Percival are knights errant in the modern wasteland that is Christendom, and what they do is the best that is done there. They are the best men in the land.

Lancelot has been detained in the Center for Aberrant Behavior, not engaged in knight errantry, but he has gradually developed a dream about knights who will clear the land of villainy. The Center is where scientific humanism deposits those whose atrocities are too horrible for adequate punishment and whose actions are "explained" reasonably as being unexplainable for which the guilty are not held responsible. Accordingly, Lancelot's crime is never punished, and he never feels guilt. Too, Percy may not want him punished.

At least five lines of narrative are important and recapitulation in some detail may clarify the author's intent: (1) Lance's confessional harangue that includes the stories of Anna and Percival, within which is Lance's (2) recapitulation of the events that led to his acts of revenge, wherein he tells (3) the story of the movie company making a picture and about (4) Elgin's home movies of activities when the film company moves from the motel back into the mansion, as well, finally, as (5) interspersed recollections of his family and of Uncle Harry. These narratives are much less complex than this enumeration may suggest and in fact are remarkably well integrated in this spare form of the *récit*.

As Lance speaks to Percival in these few days before his release from the Center, the main action is Percy's usual conflict of opinions or viewpoints and his usual concern with living death. The physical surroundings are symbolic. The setting is near a cemetery, and the time is All Souls' Day, when a great deal of physical activity goes on in the graveyard, though nothing much happens in the Center, and when all the dead souls return to haunt Lancelot. This novel, too, is a dialogue between Christian views and those of the old Southern stoic nobility.

Percy's original idea, which he freely admits didn't work, and which he gave up after a lot of unhappy effort, was to create the novel out of the dialogue between the two characters—Lancelot representing what he calls "the Southern Greco-Roman honor code" and Percival, as a childhood friend, "who has become an Augustan convert and therefore feels he has to out-Schweitzer Schweitzer," to personify the Judeo-Christian tradition. In fact Percy finds that in the mind of America today there is a refusal to accept the full implications of either code—and the diatribes of Lancelot are aimed at just this "lukewarm generalization—he despises the middle ground."[1]

Percy adds elsewhere a remark that makes him appear to support Lancelot, with whom he facetiously identifies in the self-interview mentioned in chapter one above: "The Lancelot character represents an honor code. If he had lived in the 12th century, he would have been a Crusader who believed in an idea, just as the Israelis in modern times have a noble idea."[2] That is, Lancelot's fierce revenge and his insistence on cleaning up the wasteland are aspects of the honor code.

The result of the intended dialogue would have been an undramatic theological tract in which the Christian delivered a homily and the stoic did hardly more than repeat, as Lance too elaborately does, a version of Aunt Emily's ethic in *The Moviegoer,* particularly the patrician's humanist creed about treating women gently. What is left is a narrative diatribe against the culture of Sodom, as Lance calls it, and the Christian moral failure in sexual conduct. (Lance is no longer a liberal lawyer dealing with civil rights cases.)

But the main action is Lance's recollections of the period leading to his crime. On reflection he decides he had been living in undogmatic slumber for some years, fashionably working to help blacks as a moderate liberal attorney who had begun to drink often enough to stay pleasantly comatose while his younger wife played at restoration and acting, having failed to restore him more than briefly as a part of her property. Then one day as he was about to sign a form associated with his "daughter's" plan to attend summer camp, he happened to notice that her blood type proved he could not be her father. The seven-year-old daughter of his happy ten-year-old marriage was another man's. His ordeal began with this slender perception, a mere glimmer of the mystery to be ferreted out. Binx has a similar experience when he gets onto the search, and Will operates similarly in spotting Kitty in Central Park. These are the moments that make Percy's characters come to life.

Lance says he is merely curious, but as he attempts to be reasonable about the situation, he begins to feel jealous and resentful. He also considers an apathetic decline in his family that coincides with the nation's decline. Much later he thinks there are no great events any more. His honor has been stained, whether he at once knows it or not, by an old sexual magician called Merlin. (In a kind of parallel action, his father's honor is stained because of Uncle Harry's possible affair with Lancelot's mother.) Lance reasons that only cell tissue and membranes are involved, the body and not the spirit, but somehow this purely physical interaction takes on a significance that deeply affects the mind, linking these entities as nothing else can. He is so much affected that after a good deal of talk he almost incidentally mentions jealousy and, repeatedly labeling his wife's conduct as infidelity, gradually in his recollected fury moves on to speculate that sex is a category by itself and that if sex offers the greatest happiness it is then logically the source of the greatest evil. He can thereby suggest that the concern with sex, marriage, and fidelity in the Christian framework is as important as it seems, thus the more effectively arguing the Christian view that he technically opposes.

Lancelot recalls no fury or even annoyment during the action that he recounts. Rather, he had waited and watched, very efficiently and pedantically like a lawyer as he had planned to open a nearly exhausted gas well in the basement and let the odorless methane flow into the air conditioning system. He became, as he repeatedly says, very observant of the world around him after his years of slumber and alcohol. Here, then, is a man in a concrete situation.

Lancelot lives again in this antagonistic situation, somewhat ironically in this new world, like Robinson Crusoe, as Percy presents him in the essays. His fury associates with his recollection of events and his narrative confession to Percival. In the narrative present, as he is near release from the Center, he links his deep resentment with an attack upon Christendom, a strong condemnation specifically of sexual immorality in America. He will not tolerate this condition. So strongly does he feel that he proposes a Third Revolution as an "innocent" new beginning in Virginia, where he hopes the nation will not again suffer with slavery and sexual immorality.

Lancelot's plan for the new beginning includes, of course, a new woman, for which the narrative early mentions a character never actually brought on stage. She is Anna (grace), a social worker, someone attempting humanistically to improve the condition of men who had been raped and otherwise sexually assaulted and now lies open-eyed and speechless in the adjoining cell. With her, Lancelot attempts communication by knocking on the pipes, a narrative incident that Percy uses, he says, to show the difficulty of communication. Eventually, Lancelot meets Anna, whom he considers to have regained innocence because of her ordeal and who angrily curses him for his chauvinism when he on that assumption invites her to begin anew with him. Yet, she later offers him use of property she inherits in Virginia, a corn crib and a barn, resembling Tom's slave quarters and Will's greenhouse. One of the important ideas in this story is that Lancelot does not demand a sexual virgin for himself and for Virginia, land of the Virgin. He asks only for an innocent who will not commit adultery, and he considers Anna's survival through ordeal sufficient to restore her innocence.

Another important aspect of this narrative of events of a year before is Lance's memory of his parents, the father apathetic and the mother unfaithful. The parents are also of the nobility and their antics show the absurdity of that secular condition. The father is a weak version of the romantic figure in Percy's other fiction who illustrates death in life as opposed to his son. He is the poet of Feliciana Parish (Happiness Land) who lies on the gallery, vaguely like Miniver Cheevy with his dreams of times when knights were bold, thinking about it. He has taken a bribe while in a political appointment and dreams in a rotten political situation that portends dissolution of the kingdom. Thus, what Will's father predicted of the whites has come true. Meanwhile, Lancelot's mother as Guinevere, a Southern lady somewhat more concerned than her husband is with life, enjoys the courtly attention of a cousin called Uncle Harry, who may be Lance's real father, in this narrative where, among other things, all family relationships are dubious. In a strange experience near the end of the action of the previous year, Lancelot's mother appears and gives him the knife, a phallic symbol as well as a deadly instrument, that he uses to kill the insensitive creature who has become his wife's new lover. It is the same knife that one of his sturdy masculine ancestors used for carving a man in giving quick justice to an opponent in a quarrel that ended in violence.

The activities of the movie company that plays another important role in the reminiscences produce only failure in attempted communication about human relationships and about the relationship between sex and theology, with the theme of love and life enhancement. The movie itself as a form is also a form of communication, and its message about love will be the message that the Christian nation beams out as the good news from the new world. The movie is also a form of seeing, as are the "home movies" of sexual perversion that Lancelot's squire, Elgin, a talented young black engineer, makes at Lancelot's behest to spy out the sterile secret lives of the film company.

Most important, of course, is the literal content of both the commercial movie and Elgin's movie, for their presentations of sex, love, and lust. Neither the movie company nor the movie is interesting in any sense. Lancelot scorns the group, except Merlin, his wife's first lover, the older man who probably is the father of Siobhan, the child Lance thought was his daughter. He is allowed to escape the holocaust.

The plot of the movie is ironically an account of the relationship between love and life, as also between a man and wife, paralleling also that between Lancelot's parents. But it is the perfect humanistic situation that makes a travesty of love. These are the fyttes and books and acts of the various pagan knights and the Knights of the Table Round.

Some aspects of the complex movie are important to what Percy in the self-interview calls the "sexual-theological" (L, 190) ideas of the novel. The setting is a wasteland into which a hippie Christ type comes, to revitalize by ferilizing both minds and bodies. This hero rapes, with her tacit consent, a librarian whose husband has withdrawn from life, as Lance's father has, and a white sheriff indulges with a young black woman. Members of the movie company, in a pseudo-intellectualization, claim that any erotic act is life-enhancing, thereby unwittingly devising a theory that excuses all of their sexual activities. For these people Christ died offering eternal life. Instead of accepting his offer, they talk of Christ types. But precisely this humanized mythology is what Christendom now substitutes for the living savior of Christianity. Such presumably is what Percy thinks. Besides, these film people are only mindless actors in a plot meaningless to them. The only thought is repeated: Jacoby insists on hearing the zipper. Lancelot is to conclude that the sexual act itself is violence. And in Anna, he shows what that violence does rather than enhance life.

Their private lives are waste. Here is eroticism that presumably can have no purpose except corruption of the innocent and expression of animality. These people can have no respect even for their ability to indulge in sex of whatever kind. They have no idea of the relationship between sex and life, and they have had to spend time inventing their "perversions." They are not even naturally sniffing at one another like dogs. Seeing this wasteland, and discovering that his wife willingly participates while dreaming of playing the innocent Nora in "A Doll's House," Lance decides quite simply to kill them all.

Sex and Love

But in making this decision Lance attempts to find out just what Margot did by finding out what sex is—and possibly love. Vengefully, now, one of Percy's characters wills to know what sex and man is. The theological and ontological matters such as sin and the search for the unholy grail are only comparatively important if they are significant at all. In fact, for Lancelot, who rejects Christianity as a failure in morality, the attempt to prove God's existence by finding sin is mere pomposity, or maybe this idea is a crude attempt to present the views of the silent Percival. Unfortunately, these secondary issues conceal the theme, which is original and extraordinary despite the association with an overabundance of sex during

the last three decades of this century. And Lancelot's own apparent
calm, as well as his protestation about being merely curious, conceal
until deep into the book the great injury he feels and the enormous
loss that keeps him trying to persuade Margot to remain with him.
Quite early in the action, he says what is on his mind. But when
he attempts to come to the precise statement of the question, the
puzzle, he uses a word that hardly startles or even communicates:
he says *unspeakable:* "Or is it that the sexual belongs to no category
at all, is unspeakable? Isn't sexual pleasure unspeakable? Then why
shouldn't the sexual offense be unspeakable?" (*L,* 16). Now, what
is said here is extremely important. While no logical relationship
exists between the ideas of the first two questions, between the
intensity of sexual pleasure and the seriousness of the sexual offense,
that juxtaposition is the kind of argument that Lancelot might
present. And certainly unspeakable is what the sexual pleasure is—
that is, indescribable in its intensity. It is inexpressible. Speech
cannot convey the pleasure. Once this point is clear, the point is
clearer that then one might consider the sexual offense inexpressibly
offensive. That is, language cannot describe precisely what Lancelot
wonders about: that Margot could lust and also lust after someone
besides himself. Here is *really* a difficulty in communication.[3]

What is important here, obviously, even if the idea is not at once
clear because *unspeakable* seems like an understatement, is that "the
sexual belongs to no category at all," thus is quite unlike anything
else known to human beings. To anyone with Lance's problem, this
observation is crucial. It may well bear upon or even be the secret
of life.

Lancelot knows some of the reservations too. Why, he asks his
silent friend, does anyone take the matter of fidelity seriously when
neither the Jews nor the early church bothered much about fornication and adultery? All this speculation only helps to show how
utterly unique the question, the whole situation, is for him. He
would never really understand that someone could fail to take the
matter seriously. In fact, that is his problem—attempting to understand how Margot could have been so unspeakable in what she
did. What word would explain her disregard for him and her lust
for more than one other man?

The passage is, then, by no means merely ranting, as occasional
passages appear to be: it is the central question of the novel, and
the question is what sex is. Lance wishes also to know what love

is, but what he really wants to know is the mystery of sex and its relationship to the rest of existence, especially its relationship to the mystery of life. He begins and ends with sex—why sexual attraction and the idea that sexual attraction as "rape" explains things. Not long after this passage about unspeakability, Lancelot says he has concluded that "contrary to the usual opinion, sex is not a category at all. It is not merely an item on a list of human needs like food, shelter, air, but is rather a unique ecstasy . . ." (*L,* 21).

Now, woman is at the very center of this situation. Woman is a part of the secret, of both the desire and the ecstasy. No question of equality appears to arise, for the question is how to realize the intensity of the sexual impulse and the fact that "this strange man-woman creature" is the object of desire. Lancelot is convinced really that Margot knows something he never will know about her own unspeakable desirability. In attempting to define his love for her—one of many attempts he makes throughout the novel, as he recalls the episode, not while he is blinded by jealousy during the events of the year before—he says, "she infallibly knew where the vector of desire converged, the warm cottoned-off place between her legs, the sheer negativity and want and lack where the well-fitted cotton dipped and went away" (*L,* 81). Here is the remark of a man who knows he never will know. He never will know, and for that matter he has no real conviction that Margot knows this secret that has him astounded. Altogether without ever having thought about such things, he suddenly awakes one day to the nought and the negative symbol of the blood type and finds himself involved with the mystery of being, "the sheer negativity and want and lack." The blood type itself is a mystery, as is the blood, and the conjunction of bodies and the combined cells of regeneration. A type of blood called O would be more than enough of the mystery of life if he were not overwhelmed by the larger question that possesses him.

As Lance tries to figure things out, he concludes that he has had three major experiences with love, including the sexual experiences with Margot. He compares his love for Margot with his love for his first wife Lucy. That was a romantic love. They had children, and the relationship involved sex but no mystery. He even goes so far as to consider that the course of his own history with love recapitulates somehow the history of America regarding sex, in the move from purity to permissiveness, as the moral force of Christianity declined. And a third experience with love is the developing emotion for Anna, whom he hardly knows. But he thinks her innocence has made her pure, and he wishes to have with her something resembling the love he had for Lucy as he withdraws from the absorbing indulgence with Margot and the subsequent disillusionment and loss. In attempting to distinguish loves, he says, "Lucy was a dream, a slim brown dancer in a bell jar spinning round and round in the 'Limelight' music of old gone Carolina long ago. Margot was life itself as if all Louisiana, it's fecund oil-rich dark greens and haunted twilights . . . had all . . . been gathered and fleshed out in one creature. It meant . . . holding all of goldgreen Louisiana in my arms" (L, 119).

When he remembers Lucy, he remembers her on the tennis court. And his description of her body is merely of "the way she picked up the ball." He ends this account by saying, "We were married, moved into Belle Isle, had two children. Then she died" (L, 83–84). And this, he says, was being in love—not loving but being in love. He is in love now with Anna. He does not know quite how this love for Anna resembles that of his love for Lucy, but neither is based explicitly upon sex, which he rarely mentions in talking about either of them.

But he and Margot made love on their first meeting and on their second and on and on. Gradually he realized "There was no getting enough of her. . . . There was no other thought than to possess her, as much of her with as much of me and any way at all, all ways and it seemed for always. Drinking, laughing, and loving" (L, 89–90).

To one of several inquiries from Percival, he says, "Love her? I'm not sure what words mean any more, but I loved her if loving her is wanting her all the time, wanting even the sight of her, and being away from her was like being short of breath, and seeing her . . . was a homecoming to a happy home and a rising of heart" (L, 118–19). A short time later: "Did I love her? Why are you always asking about love? . . . Margot's love was enough for me. I loved her sexually in such a way that I could not not touch her. My happiness was being with her." A few lines farther on, he says "There is no joy on this earth like falling in love with a woman. . . . Your saints say, Yes but the love of God is even better, but Jesus how could this be so? . . . And there is no pain on this earth like seeing the same woman look at another man the way she once looked at you" (*L*, 122).

In the next line, at last, he mentions jealousy: "Jealousy is an alteration in the very shape of time itself." And he has for the first time mentioned pain. These are elements in his definition of love and of the loss he feels. When Lucy died he was curious that she had been infected with an excess of white blood cells. And he has finally mentioned love of God, not, it seems, because he and Percival are arguing the point but because Lancelot wishes to define this human love as an absolute.

> You have got hold of the wrong absolutes and infinities. God as absolute? God as infinity? I don't even understand the words. I'll tell you what's absolute and infinite. Loving a woman. . . . What else is infinity but a woman become meat and drink to you, life and your heart's own music, the air you breathe? Just to be near her is to live and have your soul's own self. Just to open your mouth on the skin of her back. What joy just to wake up with her beside you in the morning. I didn't know there was such happiness. (*L*, 128–29)

He had no such happiness with Lucy, and he seems to have no idea of such happiness again, with Anna. He goes on: "But there is the dark converse: not having her is not breathing. . . . What else is man made for but this? I can see you agree about love but you look somewhat ironic. Are we talking about two different things? In any case, there's a catch. Love is infinite happiness. Losing it is infinite unhappiness" (*L*, 129).

By this point, Lancelot has linked sex and religion. His attempt to define his love for Margot and the loss he feels, a joyful positive and a dark negativity, approaches both a definition of a mystical experience of God's love and a definition of evil resembling that of St. Augustine and St. Thomas. This love for woman, which is the highest that Lancelot knows, resembles the love for God which Percival presumably has come to know. Yet the loves are different. It is just that a man who knows the one can come to know the other and then is twice blessed, presumably something like what Percival has to say when the book is done.

Now, in any case, the sexual-theological thing that Percy speaks of working at in this novel, and perhaps the others, begins to appear. Lancelot connects sex and evil: "Sin is incommensurate, right? There is only one kind of behavior which is incommensurate with anything

whatever, in both its infinite good and its infinite evil. That is
sexual behavior. The orgasm is the only earthly infinity. Therefore
it is either an infinite good or an infinite evil" (*L*, 139–40). In the
next passage, he attempts to put this intense sexual feeling within
a social context: "There is a life to be lived and a joy in living it
and the joy has nothing to do with our crazy college carryings-on
or with my crazy romantic dream of love with Lucy at Highlands.
No, it was so much simpler than that. It was simply that there is
such a thing as a beautiful day to go out into, a road to travel, good
food to eat when you're hungry, wine to drink when you're thirsty,
and most of all, 99 percent of all, no: *all* of all: a woman to love"
(*L*, 168–69). It means life is love—not God. Neither life nor love
is God. Here is phenomenological man.

Despite his ranting and his crazed recapitulation of an experience
that he had not time for rationalizing while he lived it during the
two or three days about the time of All Souls' Day the year before,
despite all his numerous shortcomings and whatever shortcomings
the narrative and the form of the book may have, Lancelot has made
love the source of the highest possible human feeling and the very
source of contemplation. No other topic is possible. Nothing else
is to be said. The subject here is love, and Lancelot finally manages
to talk about it. Even if love of God is greater, somehow, these
words, this language, about this experience describes how a man is
to feel about human love, not divine. Human love is the only divine
love. Lancelot gradually works up his definition to the point where
he defines love of woman as an absolute and the only absolute,
leaving no room for divine love.

Here, near the end of his narrative, he reveals more. While Jacoby
and Margot are making love, a voice in "prayer-like intonation"
says "God. Sh———. God. Sh———," and Lancelot asks, "Why does
love require the absolute polarities of divinity-obscenity? I was right
about love: it is an absolute and therefore beyond all categories" (*L*,
238). The extremes much resemble those of transcendent and immanent, and then what love, obscenity, and divinity have in common is more than their contiguity, as the passage goes on to suggest,
if that is important. The important fact is that the intensity of
sexual activity requires for expression something beyond any extremes, whether divinity or obscenity.

Just before the explosion, as Margot lies there like a child, appearing innocent, Lance seems to intuit a definition combining all

that he has evoked of pleasure in memories of her. She was "the only person who knew how to turn it all into love. . . . Sweetness dearness innocence singing laughing. 'Love' " (*L,* 244). He has had a dreadful experience with dread love itself. Margot gone is the divine lost, being negated. This experience is unspeakably incommunicable.

The Wasteland and the Knight

But this capacity for sex, lust, and love has its involvements for the culture, for all of humankind, especially for Christendom. The desire that possesses, the source of the longing that Percy's characters have talked about since Binx first mentioned it, or Will experienced without quite knowing what it was, that Tom recognized too well, the desire that appears with coming of age and awareness—"either it's good or it's bad," as Lancelot says. All this is forced upon his consideration when it is his own wife and his own beloved who has come to feel that lust that makes her join the whole human race and show a capacity to lust for another man—not even one other man but at least two, and who knows the end of it? And she is his wife. He already knows about his mother. When then is the end? What is going on? And he has already found out about his son, for whom sex is so plentiful that he turns to his fellowman in order to avoid the women. Siobhan is already showing her instincts. His daughter Lucy is, as he suspects, involved with Raine and Dana. So then this is Christendom.

There are only three ways to go. One is their way out there, the great whorehouse and fagdom of America. I won't have it. The second way is sweet Baptist Jesus and I won't have that. Christ, if heaven is full of Southern Baptists, I'd rather rot in hell with Saladin and Achilles. There is only one way we could have had it if you Catholics hadn't blown it: the old Catholic way. . . . Then we knew what a woman should be like, your Lady, and what a man should be like, your Lord. I'd have fought for your Lady, because Christ had the broadsword. Now you've gotten rid of your Lady and taken the sword from Christ. (*L,* 176–77)

Jealous as Lancelot may be, what enrages him is the infidelity— that of Margot his wife, that of his mother, and that of American culture. (Percy is no longer concerned with the West.) He can persuade himself that sexual intercourse is only the friction of molecules, and thus understand what Margot has done, but he cannot find a reason for the infidelity itself—the unfaithfulness, that personal disregard for him that allowed her to enjoy *lovemaking* with Merlin, another man to whom she was not married.

Margot's infidelity is for Lancelot far more than the mere act of interaction of molecules. It is also a denial of his being, encouraged in a culture that shows *The 69ers* and *Deep Throat* openly and legally in movie theaters. In addition, he has known nothing of her infidelity, and she explicitly denies it at a crucial moment before the murders occur, at a time when he is yet willing, despite his injured pride, to ignore his honor for the sake of his love, deliberately, not in apathy as his father had done, but deliberately choosing love over honor.

Lance blames women far more than men for the immorality because they have allowed themselves to give so freely. There are no ladies anymore; all women are whores, including his mother. He rages with profane vulgarity about the voraciousness of the female appetite. Yet he also claims to have discovered at last the secret that generations keep from one another: the sexual assault.

Women have only just now discovered the secret, or part of it, the monstrous absurdity of it . . . that their happiness and the meaning of life itself is to be assaulted by a man . . . to be rammed, jammed, stuck, stabbed, pinned, impaled, run through, in a word:
    Raped. (*L,* 222–23)

Lance's Plan

The plan for the Third Revolution to begin in old Virginia is quite simply for a violent cleansing of manners and mores, in sex particularly, that will restore a moral code resembling the one that Christians have abandoned. It will be strict and severe. Lance's main point is that he will not "tolerate this age" of sexual indulgence. No matter what his own involvement in the age, his experiences with Margot and the movie people have showed him "the lost people" of Dante's Purgatory mentioned in the novel's epigraph. (Actually, he has been faithful during his marriage with Margot, and his vulgar concession to Raine's lust just before he kills Jacoby has nothing to do with sexual conduct. It is only vulgarity and violence. He is possibly telling the truth when he says that love is hate and in then showing his hatred through his obscene buggery of Raine.)

At the heart of the moral code are two ideas: honor and love, the old chivalric ideas. The honor will be the kind that does not accept bribes. In fact, all men will be gentlemen whose conduct will coincide with their stations and positions. These will also be men of action. Lancelot will, in short, have no one resembling either of his parents or his Uncle Harry.

More important, if possible, men will respect women. The distinction between ladies and whores will be clear—in the way women present themselves and in the way men respond to them. It is important to recognize that Lancelot has no interest in understanding what Margot appears to want him to understand—that lady and whore are false distinctions. He wants precisely to know whether a woman is a lady or a whore and respond to her accordingly. He does not want sex to be available at any time and place from any woman. He does not want whores or anything resembling them. He wants in fact to know that a woman is faithful and virginal. "The New Woman will have perfect freedom," he says. "She will be free to be a lady or a whore" (*L,* 179). The point must be made that Margot's remark that he always wanted her to be either lady or whore is abrupt and unexpected. She made herself a whore. The narrative gives no indication that Lancelot ever has been unfaithful to either wife or immoral in any other way. He discounts premarital sex for himself and Percival. He may not ultimately disapprove of the homosexual couple, and his point about his son is woman's lust. He does not even protest the way Raine and Dana treat his daughter Lucy.

Such is the statement of his strong feelings. But, he says, now that his harangue is done, he will "give your God time," convinced that God also will no longer tolerate this. That is, Lancelot and Percival agree about the abandon of the age. And offering to give God another chance when God has had years of "chance" is ridiculous. What else can Lance do? Further, his intention to form a new culture is an accompaniment of his raging. He had thought nothing as he planned the explosion. He had no plans for a future. Opening the lantern before he buggered Raine must mean that he "planned" suicide.

It is his opinion that all is lost with the failure of Christendom now that we are living in the "whorehouse and fagdom of America."

Gentlemen must begin to recognize one another by a "stern code:
a gentleness toward women and an intolerance of swinishness, a
counsel kept, and above all a readiness to act, and act alone if
necessary" (L, 157) with "stern rectitude valued by the new breed
and marked by the violence which will attend its breach" (L, 158).
Here is the explanation of his murders of the "lost people."

And he goes on for Percival: "Then how shall we live if not with
Christian love? One will work and take care of one's own, live and
let live, and behave with a decent respect toward others. If there
cannot be love—you call that love out there?—there will be a tight-
lipped courtesy between men. And chivalry toward women. Women
must be saved from the whoredom they've chosen. Women will
once again be strong and modest. Children will be merry because
they will know what they are to do" (L, 158–59). Elsewhere he
says, "There will be men who are strong and pure of heart, not for
Christ's sake but for their own sake. There will be virtuous women
who are proud of their virtue . . ." (L, 178).

What Lancelot wants in distinguishing between lady and whore
and in conceiving of courteous men of action is the ideal of the Lord
and Lady, rejecting of course the courtly love tradition and distinguishing between two aspects of human nature—the love for woman
as wife and the indulgence of sex, with woman being blamed.

Percy does not reject Lancelot. He writes Lancelot's tirade. He
rejects Lancelot's plan. He accepts the shriven Lancelot's offer to
wait upon God. Here Percy particularly enjoys asking if it is the
crazy man who is crazy.

Percival

In some of the Grail romances (Wolfram's *Parzival* at least) Percival was for some reason warned against curiosity and against talking too much. The result was failure to ask the question that would
have led to restored health for the maimed king. Whether this
aspect of the legends encouraged Percy to silence Percival or not,
Percival's role as interlocutor is relatively slight. (And whether the
interlocutor's comic association with Mr. Bones explains Lancelot's
reference to Percival's bundle of bones may be irrelevant.) But Percival does persist in a question that has all possible significance for
healing Lancelot. "Did you love her?" Lancelot says Percival keeps
asking, and in part for this reason Lancelot continues to reply with

increasing attempts to express the love he felt. He does then finally
say how he loved her, and in doing so—loving her—he shows all
the deficiency in his love of God. Here is another aspect of the Grail
romance so important here. Love of woman supersedes love of God.
Sex is everything God is not. Percy becomes gradually more mys-
tified by the mystery of sexual attraction, the force of the sex instinct,
and the intensity of sexual pleasure. He will devote the next novel
to the matter also.

Lancelot speaks for the love of women, and Percival is silent in
the love of God. In the age of chivalry evoked in their names,
Lancelot represented courtly love and Percival the quest for divine
love. The novel, in becoming not a dialogue literally but a statement
of Lancelot's view, investigates, analyzes, anatomizes earthly love.
But what Percival has left to tell Lancelot when the novel ends is
the story of divine love. Actually, both the romantic falling in love
associated with Lancelot's first wife Lucy and the joyous sexual
indulgence with Margot are aspects of the old courtly love tradition
that Lancelot's name calls up. Ideal and real are combined in the
offer of the knight's services to his lady's whims, but the real is in
her eventual disposal of her favors on him.

What Percival has left to tell Lancelot is, of course, everything
he has not heard. Lancelot has been through hell and purgatory.
Percival will talk to him about Paradise, as the apostle with authority
to speak of the grace of God. When the Percival of the romances
got the second chance, he performed the deed that ended the suffering. He asked what the trouble was and set in motion the divine
process of salvation.

Lancelot is somewhat like Will in perceiving rather late in his
narrative when he is nearly finished that "You know something you
think I don't know" (*L,* 256), and they agree that things as they
are will not do. But Percival, the anonymous Father John, former
whoremonger, converted, who plans to take an impoverished living
in Alabama, is a changed man with a message. Whatever his past
was, he is ordained to tell men of the heavenly city and the way of
salvation. This message is always new and "unknown" until presented. He will make his little contribution. He could speak with
the "authority" that Lance talks about. He, however, awaits an act
of penance after the confession so that he can deliver the blessing.
He has then everything to say about life and love, all that is important to man. While Lancelot invokes a vengeful God, Percival

prepares to speak of God's love. He has already decided to go to the anonymous service in a little church in Alabama. In bringing God to them when Lancelot finishes, Percival arranges for *Lancelot* also to have a happy ending.

Chapter Nine
The Second Coming

The sad old world has come to such a state that Will Barrett, if he were a believer, would believe the second coming were at hand. Will is a latter day Binx, sick of the world and the "suck of self" (*SC*, 14), with a malady of discontent he has inherited from his father. He returned from Santa Fé after watching Jamie's deathbed baptism, as recorded in *The Last Gentleman,* where the ritualized epiphany left him in another fugue state. Instead of marrying Kitty, however, as the end of *The Last Gentleman* appeared to suggest he would, he became a Wall Street lawyer, dealing not with human rights but with estates and trusts for the wealthy. He married a great deal of money and later began to worry that he chose the money instead of being a gentleman when he married a homely rich girl. Marion, the woman, a religious heiress with a polio limp, dies of jaundice and leaves him with a burden of good causes, a born-again daughter, a mild generation gap, and a life to live. Sutter, of course, came to nothing. He talks only during television commercials and waits for his pension check, still in Albuquerque.

When the novel opens, Will has retired early from law practice and lives in a small town in North Carolina, not quite the South of the other novels, since here the "Negro Question" has never been asked. He is the most accomplished golf amateur of them all, but he suddenly begins playing badly; and when he does, he begins to awake from years of dozing, much as Lancelot did, to discover that he has never lived and that life is on the end of ordeal. Depression seems the most likely cause of his troubles, but he also blacks out. He is obsessed with the idea that the Jews may be leaving North Carolina and the country in accordance with the prophecy that Jews must be gathered to their homeland and converted to Christianity in anticipation of the second coming of Christ to judgment of the world for its sins. Will is sick in body, mind, and spirit, with a malaise more intense than Binx experienced.

Associated with these difficulties is another mental disturbance, the attempt of hidden memories to reappear and explain much he does not know he has forgotten. This technique, used somewhat in *The Last Gentleman* and more emphatically in *Lancelot,* maintains a degree of suspense in a spare plot and finally explains Will's relationship to his father and to life—death-in-life—which has characterized his attitudes since he was twelve and experienced a hunting "accident," when his father tried to kill him. Will lives under his old theory that people are unhappy in good environments and, during the first 250 pages of the novel, considers proving it by commiting suicide. Meanwhile, he indulges an alternative transcendent *ism* by deciding to sacrifice himself for believers and unbelievers alike, for neither of which he has any respect, in forcing God either to reveal himself or to reveal his nonexistence. This feat of angelism Will expects to perform all immanently underground, by descending into a cave where he will die unless God rescues him.

A parallel action deals with Allison, a neurotic girl of twenty, who is Kitty's daughter, just escaped from a hospital for the mentally ill. She and most of the other characters in this novel are lame and halt, mentally disturbed, born again to excesses or otherwise deficient, those for whom salvation was originally devised. All the main characters—Will, Allison, Marion, and Will's daughter—were injured as children, usually by disease, though Percy never shows much overt concern with such matters. Allison has an inheritance from an unlikely source and moves into an abandoned greenhouse on a piece of the property she inherited. This coincidental enterprise aids the denouement, when all the mentally and physically mangled are called out of sick bays and retirement homes to participate in life until death occurs, as a part of the natural process of living activity and not from desuetude. In the end Will and Allison, as unlikely a couple as ever were invented, discover each other by falling in love. Percy's fifth novel also has a happy ending with a marriage.

Attack on Christendom

This novel is yet another attack on Christendom, in the most religious town in the most religious state in the most religious section of the most religious country in the world. Percy gives the impression that it has all become a little too dull even to satirize, as if the facts themselves were caricature. He juxtaposes two priests in order to show the old values and the new. One is Jack Curl, an Episcopal priest who has trouble saying that he believes in God, choosing to live a lie rather than tell one. He has adopted all the reforms of the Episcopal church, and he respects the plethora of sects and splinter groups with a paucity of religion. He is in the tradition of the fat friar, with revised liturgy, reform, and social welfare. He wants to help everybody. Except for his retreats (ironically held in Billy Graham's Montreat, with a fine ecumenicity that voids the truth by accepting all disagreements as meaningless), he has little to do with wayfaring. Rather, he is extending Christendom by attempting to establish love communities and retirement villages with, for example, the "charming" idiot performers Tod and Tannie, singing while "Crosswits" is on the silent television set. (These may be the sexual performers, Ted and Tanya, from *Love in the Ruins,* his name now a form of *death.*)

On the other hand, Father Weatherbee (who presumably has been weathered in the service of his God) has been doing the evangelical and missionary work of the church for years, not in a "happy" and well-funded community in North Carolina but in the outcountry of Mindanao. Despite his appearance and his manner, which appear to make him decrepit if not obscene, he is the apostle who delivers the news, which people believe because he took the trouble to tell them. The islanders had their simple love and morality community as compared with Jack Curl's dream of a rich love and faith community. Couples remained chaste until Father Weatherbee joined them in matrimony.

Instead of juxtaposing stoic and Roman Catholic positions, as he has done in *Lancelot* and *The Moviegoer,* Percy takes up again the dialectic of *The Last Gentleman,* that of believers and unbelievers. Here goes everybody, somewhat as in *Love in the Ruins.* The tone is generally calm, especially as compared with *Lancelot,* which makes the novel appear thin. But Will, like Binx, includes most of the United States among those he finds living the inauthentic existence called death-in-life. Much less burdened with philosophy and theology than the other novels, especially *Lancelot,* which by immediately preceding it invites comparison, this novel brings to a conclusion in unity the puzzling matter of love that Percy began to study implicitly in his first novel.

Watching has finally at least led Will to this devout priest. But before this good fortune occurs, Will makes a simultaneous search and quest, something not heretofore seen in Percy's work, unless Binx's search for his father was in some way also a search for authority.

The Two Fathers

Of the two fathers, one is heavenly and one is earthly. And Will accepts neither, so no atonement occurs, even if Will eventually places himself in the way of accepting grace.

The concern with the father expressed in other Percyean quests apparently is resolved in this novel, however. In a series of episodes running through the greater portion of the action, Will tries to disperse a cloud of unknowing that conceals what he concludes he has always known, that his metaphysically restive father tried to kill them both. The musing is unfortunately, perhaps unavoidably, Faulknerian, even if the theme is more appropriate to Percy.

But in this novel the concern with the father seems more nearly central to the hero's actions than in others. After days of musing, at first without quite realizing that his father is the problem, Will sees that his father was trying to save him from the anguish of boredom in a world where God is perniciously ambiguous about himself. (Percy manages to avoid sentimentality after setting the stage for it.) Will concludes that his father too richly wished to die and reacts at once against his father's position. In part because of his growing love for Allison (and the concomitant rejuvenation), he defies the shade of his father, and chooses life.

Actually Will chose life in *The Last Gentleman,* in opposing Sutter's will to cease to be and in planning to return to Kitty. But now, amid references to hoisting—lifting up—and growth, plants, greenhouses, hydroponic beans, and natural air in the steady temperature of the underground, he chooses life as the natural act in the natural world, where so many wonders are. He was himself thinking much about suicide, with his father's guns around during most of the action, but he throws them, his heritage of death, into a chasm where they are lost forever in the abyss, the realm of death. The choice for life after pages of Proustian musing about the past is rather impressive and believable, though the novel makes too much of the sweet release when Will and Allison go to the motel to make love. And what Will chooses is life, not eternal life, with this action.

Precisely at this living, however, they both have failed. Allison says that she made A's in school but failed at living. She could not function when watched or expected to function. The result is a structured life with structured electrical shocks until she finally discovers herself free to choose an unstructured existence in which she acts and performs. Her vague hope is to "get away from my everlasting self sick of itself to be with another self and is that what *it* is?" (*SC,* 257) and "is loving you . . . the be-all not end-all?" (*SC,* 258). (The *it* she mentions here refers to her unclear perception of some combination of sex and love.)

Will has nothing else to do, so he thinks he had as well use up his own worthless existence to force God to prove His existence. He rejects the earthly father and pursues the heavenly father, though he expects little from either course of action. He has no idea even of being a hero or recovering being. Though he is an unbeliever in Christendom, at least until the end of the novel, he will descend underground, there confront the shades, the mysteries, and his spiritual father and require of Him a blessing. As a seeker after truth, he goes on behalf of both groups: believers, like "fifteen million Southern Baptists," populate Christendom and "are repellent precisely to the degree that they embrace and advertise that truth" (*SC,* 188). But the unbeliever, scientist and humanist, the educated generally, is worse "because of the fatuity, blandness, incoherence, fakery, and fatheadedness of his unbelief " (*SC,* 189). Yet, Will and Percy speak directly to the educated unbeliever: "born into a world of endless wonders, having no notion how he got here, a world in which he eats, sleeps, shits, fucks, works, grows old, gets sick, and dies, and is quite content to have it so. Not once in his entire life does it cross his mind to say to himself that his situation is preposterous, that an explanation is due him and to demand such an explanation and to refuse to play out another act of the farce until an explanation is forthcoming" (*SC,* 189). But Will intends at least to put the question, as he tells Sutter in his suicide note, ironically a long epistle to the Laodiceans. He will not choose death as his father did or bet on God's existence, as Pascal suggests, or merely have faith. He devises a hero's way of putting the question to deity—"a situation in which one's death would occur if and only if God did not manifest himself, did not give a sign clearly and unambiguously, once and for all" (*SC,* 192). "My experiment," he adds, "is simply this: I shall go to a desert place and wait for God to give a sign. If no sign is forthcoming I shall die. But people will know why I died: because there is no sign. The cause of my death will be either his nonexistence or his refusal to manifest himself, which comes to the same thing as far as we are concerned" (SC, 193).

Will's simplicity is stunning. And while his logic may be flawless, it has nothing to do with reality—not with toothaches or with the immense pride he never recognizes. But the toothache—the pain— or nausea, as Percy decides to name the immanence, brings him from this transcendental apperception back to the real world. Some- where along the way of his wandering he concludes: "There are two secrets to life nobody tells you: screwing and dying. What they tell you about is love and the hereafter. Maybe they are right. But it is screwing and dying you have to deal with. What they don't tell you is how good screwing is and how bad it is to grow old, get sick, and die" (SC, 218–19). This is one of the visions that Will has as he lies in wait for God in Sourwood Mountain. This theme of love and death is repeated in the major actions of Will's life, the shooting "accident," the experience with Allison, his life with Mar- ion, until he and Allison find a union in love and life.

In a handsome litany for the dead that appears after his defeat in the bowels of the earth, Will rejects all the confetti of life and Christendom.

Death in the guise of belief is not going to prevail over me, for believers now believe anything and everything and do not love the truth, are in fact in despair of the truth, and that is death.

Death in the guise of unbelief is not going to prevail over me, for unbelievers believe nothing, not because truth does not exist but because they have already chosen not to believe and would not believe, cannot believe, even if the living truth stood before them, and that is death. (SC, 272–73)

He rejects Christendom and Christianity, old and new, and love as he has known it. He especially rejects marriage, family, and chil- dren, and all the virtues. Finally, he says, "Death in the form of isms and asms shall not prevail over me, orgasm, enthusiasm, lib- eralism, conservatism, Communism, Buddhism, Americanism, for an ism is only another way of despairing of the truth" (SC, 273). This last observation is a composite of the ills that Tom feared from angelism, and they are the usual half-gods that men attempt to substitute for God.

The outburst, culminating his period of depression as well as his discernment of his father's intention to kill him as a way of relieving him of the worldweariness of life, is dramatic in its undertone. It concerns more than Percy has openly criticized and leaves only the "truth seeker," sounding a little like one of Nietzsche's outbursts: *"But at least protest. . . . What is missing? God? Find him!"* (*SC*, 273). Here is another echo of Binx the truthseeker (*M*, 14), from twenty years ago in Percy's career.

None of Lancelot's shouting so eloquently approaches the statement of despair or so urgently edifies. This novel, like all the others, refrains from evangelism, yet it is possibly more anxious than any of the others about fostering its message of spirituality and renewal. This renewal comes through God's grace in offering love of both kinds. In this novel finally Percy rejoins body and soul.

Love

Quite early in the action Allison asks what love is (*SC*, 39), and she wanders through the usual questions about sex until she falls in love with Will. Will himself is unconcerned with love, so little concerned that he fails to recognize it anywhere, until nearly too late. He did not love his wife and appears unconcerned about his daughter. That may be the point—that he has forgotten love— everybody has forgotten love. Will has merely performed his duty during all the years. The youthful Allison, having escaped death-in-life on her initiative and having "fallen in love at first sight," does speculate, however, and that keeps the theme there for Will when he at last awakens.

Allison has indulged in all the sexual techiques found in her first lover's picturebook, but she wonders what IT is, and she ponders whether a relationship exists between "doing it" and "being in love." The question, thus neatly phrased in the vernacular, has considerable importance for the semireligious matter of interpersonal subjectivity (loving another), that Percy studies here. A comparison with Binx and Kate illuminates this matter, though Tom and Ellen led the way. Binx and Kate have only an interpersonal relationship and Binx is understood to be religious, but Kate is not convincingly worth his trouble. And sex is not mentioned after the failure on the train (or Aunt Emily's lecture). But in *The Second Coming,* that severe puritanic restraint opens out on explicit scenes of sexual love in which Allison resolves her questions, with Will's enthusiastic agreement. What happens is a combination of the aspects of human love, a synthesis of Tom's analysis. In a song, Allison says, "The lover is asking a brook to carry his message of love to a maiden" (*SC,* 354), in what is the most usual form of romantic love with a courtly sexual undertone. And in a beautiful dialogue that becomes gradually explicit, Allison says she thinks Will has something for her and asks what. Will, perhaps only now realizing what is the word he wants and what the thing is, says, " 'Love. I Love you. . . . I love you now and until the day I die' " (*SC,* 355). No character in Percy's world has ever said it or said it so simply and beautifully. The point needs repeating. Lancelot may have been close, in the raw circumstances after he has killed Jacoby when he feels a sad tenderness for Margot. But no character in Percy's work has ever said *love.* Will, however, is more explicit, finally, at the author's urging, after Binx's attempts at immanence and Sutter's speculations about lewdness and Tom's near resolution and Lancelot's nearly instinctive murder for the sake of being. Finally, Will explicitly joins the polarities: " 'I love your dearest heart. I also love your dear ass' " (*SC,* 355). Ironically, this observation had to wait upon the permissiveness of the society of the sixties and seventies. But at least in love they are reborn, Allison immanent, Will transcendent, Allison speaking in tongues their holy idiocy, Will listening at last without deafness.

The extent to which this incident expresses Percy's personal opinion may be clear from a passage that appears in the self-interview published in 1977, about the time he must have begun work on *The Second Coming.* He says,

Then, if he is near someone he loves or wants to love or should love or perhaps has loved all along but has not until this moment known it, he looks at her. And by exactly the same measure by which the novel has opened to him and he to it, he opens to her and she to him. Well now, why don't you come here a minute? That's it. Give me your hand. He looks at her hand. He is like the castaway on the beach who opens his eyes and sees a sunrise coquina three inches from his nose. Her hand is like the coquina. What an amazing sight! Well now, why don't we just sit down here on this cypress log? Imagine your being here at four-thirty in the afternoon. All this time I thought I was alone on this island and here you are. A miracle! Imagine Crusoe on his island performing the ultimate stunt for his goats, when he turns around there *she* is. (184, 186)

What all this is above all and aside from all and in addition to all is life—the joy of living.

Their love makes them think of others, and they set about building their own little Eden. It will have an unstructured natural environment, a greenhouse with a constant temperature provided by nature, and it will grow living things. (It will even, like the swamps of the reformed Faust, furnish housing for people—young couples.) Will plans to give all he has to the poor, though ironically he marries potential wealth again. The community he plans, a third after Jack Curl's planned obsolescence complex and Father Weatherbee's Christian one in Mindanao, will include two builders with failing limbs and an old man who waters lonesome pines, as well as an assortment of wanderers, emigrés, and homeless. All the forlorn will be there. They will be set to work tending the garden, all of it quite natural and in the concrete world, where they will love and labor until they die. A comparison of this green and happy land with Lancelot's grandiose madness ought to show where Percy was really going.

Place and Time

The Second Coming is actually a collection of interlinked symbols rather than simply a narrative revelation of events making up a plot. Language and communication, the relationship between body and soul, and the two kinds of love are major themes. And at the heart of the collection are the integrated themes of love-death and time-place. The *theme* of time-place is so important that nearly any mention of either time or place is automatically a part of the *symbolism* of time-place. The conjunction is precise; facts about time and place are immediately also symbols.

The novel opens on space, though the main action occurs within the limited perimeter of the golf course. Will falls and looks up at the sky with the "cumulous cloud . . . towering thousands of feet into the air," and this is the "first time he admitted to himself that something might be wrong" (*SC*, 3). The narrative moves on to mention hole 17, a "medium-long dogleg with a good view of Sourwood Mountain" (*SC*, 5), naming in "dogleg" the first angle of the narrative. With this incident of expectations gone awry, Will awakes to adventure and ordeal. In the same paragraph, with mention of "an event that happened a long time ago" (*SC*, 3), death is introduced, though Will's refusal to remember leaves the subject unspoken. Nature is described again as the background for action here, then an odor recalls for Will a series of incidents with Ethel Rosenblum that introduces sexual love, leaving it, too, unnamed until one of Will's doctors locates the difficulty in a space in the brain—"near the brain's limbic system, seat of all desire, a location which would account for the sexual component of his disorder" (*SC*, 8). The time was specifically when he was fifteen. Soon, then, Will has a place of love and a place of death, and the two with variants recur throughout the narrative until his love for Allison removes his desire for death.

Speculation about one aspect of both time and place begins quite early in the novel and deals with one of Percy's favorite topics. Will questions: "Was there ever truly uneventful time, years of long afternoons when nothing happened and people were glad of it?" (*SC*, 16). He gives up the subject of time for a "revelation" about place. He has just noticed a cat: "Sitting there in the sun with its needs satisfied, for whom one place was the same as any other place as long as it was sunny—no nonsense about old haunted patches of weeds in Mississippi or a brand-new life in a brand-new place in Carolina—the cat was exactly a hundred percent cat, no more no less." But people nowadays "occupied a place uneasily and more or less unsuccessfully." Often they were mere "specters who hardly occupied a place at all" (*SC*, 16).

Will has the essential problems with time and place. Where is he to spend a lifetime? The question of what to do at four o'clock in the afternoon is nearly crucial to both Will and Allie, such that when they fall in love, Will promises to be with her at that time every day. In addition, Will has yet to find a place and to decide what to do with the rest of his life. In fact, if he fails to find a place, he will likely commit suicide, locating himself in the grave for all time, as his father has done. He moves in extremes throughout the novel, shifting symbolically and sometimes literally between swamp and attic, in keeping with the lifting imagery, as he moves from the swamp where the hunting "accident" occurred to the attic where his father killed himself. Much of the action is set off by his Proustian memory of the Georgia swamp when he searches for the golf ball in the rough near Allie's greenhouse. As he finally moves through that place and that action again and again, trying to recall what happened, he gradually moves upward onto his own ledge above the cove and into the attic where his father died and to the second story of his own house in North Carolina where he finds the guns in the closet.

Allie is looking for a literal place when the novel opens, an old homeplace earlier belonging to someone else; and she has just escaped a place of confinement to discover she has freedom of action. She is unaware of time in knowing neither date nor years. Her calendar is the wrong year and she decides against buying a Timex watch. (Will later buys one for himself.) She even has a map to use for locating her property.

She works throughout the few weeks of the action to make the place habitable, to trim it and heat it. That is her function, and she gets herself and it to the point where she can tell the doctor that the injured Will is at her "what?—'place' " (*SC,* 249). She has worried over the problem of making merry without a home. And she has defined a home as "a place, any place, any building, where one sinks into one's self and finds company waiting" (*SC,* 242). Meanwhile, she has invitations to places offering religion and sex, important components of the home. A woman with a smile, more resembling Lamia than an angel, invites her to an "address . . . stamped on the back" (*SC,* 33). It sounds like a furtive meeting for some forbidden fruit. Then a young man invites her to a personal encounter in a shack on the Appalachian Trail. But she has "to locate and take possession of a house" (*SC,* 36).

Will meanwhile has nothing but houses, hostels, hospitals, and homes (for sick, maimed, aged, everyone but himself)—yet, finally, his house empty and his home forlorn, he takes Allie to a motel because he has no home anywhere in Christendom, though he owns a considerable part of the most religious spot in the world. "I dont live anywhere," he says (*SC,* 332).

Place and time for both Will and Allie ultimately are facts of life—the conditions of their new life together and of their intention to live under an intended marriage that is really a pact for life—to engage in living life instead of ending it. Coming to know Will, falling in love, planning marriage and family are for Allison coming to know "what to do with the rest of her life" (*SC,* 31).

This theme and its relationship to the theme of love and death is treated in yet more detail in *The Second Coming.* Will's concern with place is elaborate. It involves a mysterious beginning with a triangular plot of land that is probably intended to suggest the woman's triangular center of life and love-death—"a weedy stretch . . . a wedge-shaped salient of weeds angling off between the railroad tracks and the back yards of Negro cabins. It was shaped like a bent triangle, the bend formed by the curve of tracks. . . . in one corner there was a small fenced and locked enclosure which contained an even smaller metal hut" (SC, 7). On the next page he says, "Ethel, let's me and you homestead this leftover land here and now, this nonplace, this surveyor's interstice" (SC, 8). The place is memorable because it was the location of Will's first encounter with desire, Ethel Rosenblum, ugly of face, his first Jew also, but fine of limb and lucid mentally. She managed to cancel out all the contradictions and unknowns and offer unity, which, however, Will passed up in the brief encounter with a few meager, evasive words and there chose death over love. Then he regrets he never said to her "Ethel . . . I know a place" (SC, 9). Ethel of course also knew the place Will sought, though he was not to find it for many years thereafter. It was home when he did. This place and the swamp in Georgia where his father shot him and left him watchful are the two places in his recollections. One has to do with love and the other with death, the screwing and dying that he finds at the heart of existence: "Did you not then believe, old mole, that these two things alone are real, loving and dying, and since one is so much like the other and there is so little of the one, in the end there remained only the other?" (SC, 162).

The specific link with dying occurs as Will returns home from his father's funeral (an incident which he remembers as he goes home from his wife's funeral). "When the limousine stopped at the railroad crossing . . . a nondescript place he had passed a hundred times walking home from school, he noticed that this place had a different look, an air of suspension, of pause and hiatus. . . . This was the same place where he had thought about Ethel Rosenblum and fallen down" (SC, 219). Will's consistent falling during the greater part of the narrative is one of the reasons for Allison's point that she hoists. This link between sex and death is repeatedly made in the novel. It is found even in a contrived incident near the end in which a white woman is succored by two blacks in a hospital as they more or less make an assignation. And with Marion Will spends much time going to funerals while nothing is said of their love life.

This place or some variant of it reappears in Will's thoughts throughout the novel. He later realizes that "It was the very sort of place, a nondescript weedy triangular public pubic sort of place, to make a sort of love or to die a sort of death" (*SC*, 162). Later, a long passage deals with place and time as Will dreams (*SC*, 275–77), then yet later he manages to forget the place in exorcizing his demon. He "lives" with Allie at the Holiday Inn for two days. There "The slot in the drapes showed a corner of the Holiday Inn property. The corner was empty, no pool, no lounges, no tables, no cars, no children's playground. Yet the grass was well trimmed up to the fence separating it from the pasture. He wondered how many people had set foot in this empty corner over the years. Perhaps none" (*SC*, 336). Within the next few minutes, he casts both guns, the Greener the symbol of death and the Lüger the symbol of love death, from the overlook. He "went away without listening," watching, or waiting. The next section begins with "It was light." Allie wakes him from the protection of fetal sleep in which he dreamed of the Georgia swamp and he notices the "unused ungrazed . . . corner" (*SC*, 338), then calls on Allison to turn to him. For the first time they make love. "There was an angle but it did not make trouble. Entering her was like turning a corner and coming home" (*SC*, 339). This observation, with its puns, its metaphors, and its simple fact, is the resolution of symbolism, theme, and lifelong problem for Will. Percy soon thereafter "moves" them into a garden home.

What Percy wishes to accomplish in the distortion of time is unclear, but he obviously wishes to shift from concentration on memory and the past with its unpleasant associations to the future. As quoted elsewhere, Will says near the end of the book, " 'I love you now and until the day I die' " (*SC*, 355). The long passage dealing with place (cited but not quoted above) begins with a reference to time, as Will settles to sleep in the back of his Mercedes: "This is what is going to happen." The author adds "In the very moment of sinking into a deep sleep he had, not a dream or a flight of fancy, but a swift sure unsurprised presentiment of what lay in store" (*SC*, 274). What follows is a series of views of a place during a period of time—it is a desert place at beginning and end of Will's experience, so often the case with Percy's main characters. And the passage ends: "When he came to years from now, he was lying on the spot" (*SC*, 277). He awakes and finds Kitty with another threat of sex. (The passage ends with a series of (probably) famous last words, among them "Rosebud," attributed to William Randolph Hearst, and "the great distinguished thing," attributed to Henry James.) A curious one-line paragraph follows: "The ocean was not far away" (*SC,* 277). It vaguely recalls a similarly curious incident in *The Last Gentleman* when Will wanders off to Flatbush and has a nap on the shore.

As noted above in the discussion of *The Last Gentleman,* Percy says he used Eric Voegelin's remarks about time in his outline of Will's distortions. A passage from Voegelin's *Ecumenic Age* may help to explain what Percy wishes to accomplish here. Mentioning Eliade's *Mythe de l'eternel retour,* Voegelin says,

It is the field of the previously mentioned rituals of renewal that has, as Eliade observes, the function of abolishing time, of undoing its waste and corruption, and of returning to the pristine order of the cosmos through a repetition of the cosmogonic act. He speaks of the purpose of the New Year rituals . . . as the attempt to bring becoming to a standstill, to restore being to the ordered splendor that is lethally flowing away with the flow of time. . . . The experience of a cosmos existing in precarious balance on the edge of emergence from nothing and return to nothing must be acknowledged, therefore, as lying at the center of the primary experience of the cosmos. [1]

If Percy did roll this heavy weight into his novel, he may have accomplished less than one could hope for. Kitty's "light" obfuscates.

These few observations do not exhaust the uses of time and place in *The Second Coming.* A thorough study might reveal much. And the number of memorable places may be higher in this novel than in any of the others. Among them are the proposed love-and-faith community as well as the home where Will stays for awhile, the greenhouse, closet, bus, the pittosporum limb where Allie overhears talk of her future, the various hospital rooms, the motel room, the triangular corner in its various stages, the springhouse, the cove, the summerhouse, the cave, and of course the back seats of the cars. Previous use as a tiger's lair and hiding place for Confederate soldiers gives longevity to the place where Will decides to have his confrontation with God. And finally, of course, the second coming itself, at the hour and time unknown, would be time and place.

Epiphany

The most remarkable aspect of *The Second Coming* is its ending. Percy has ended all his novels unexpectedly with a miracle of sorts, actually with an epiphany—God appears. Binx suddenly is religious, Jamie's death reveals the miracle of baptism and salvation, Tom confesses, takes the Eucharist, and celebrates God's presence. After Lancelot's raving about meaninglessness, Percival offers the alternative of eternal life, and, finally, here, almost too suddenly even to crown the efforts of the seeker after truth, Will awakes to far more than he knew to wish for.

Percy has always had the problem of attempting to write the Christian and Roman Catholic novel without being evangelical. So Will ponders the deadness of life and worries about God's existence without revealing much personal concern. And this novel, like others, dwells on the question of love, the rift in body and soul, and the queerness of unhappy man in good environments.

Finally, in the last three sections of *The Second Coming*, Percy finds a resolution. Section 10 begins after Will has arranged for the three old men to go to work for him and Allison and he goes to find Father Weatherbee to ask him to perform the religious marriage ceremony he has decided on. What is more important, he has found the man he wants for the ceremony. While delayed by "a big florid fellow" (*SC*, 351) who deplores councils on aging and insists Will should hang on to his money, Will says, " 'I just thought of something.' . . . He was backing away. He had to find her. His need of her was as simple and urgent as drawing the next breath" (*SC*, 353).

Juxtaposition and jointure are so important here that Percy breaks into the narrative and sends Will off to Allison for all her love and back then to Father Weatherbee, so that human love will come first then divine love. In section 11, Will comes upon Allison in the sunlight singing "Love's Message" and planting avocados. They move through a language game, both eloquent now, he no longer deaf and she no longer dumb, to where he says, " 'I love you now and until the day I die' " (*SC*, 355), then moves on to make love and to speak at more length. Coming after the section dramatizing their sexual encounter, this scene is nearly pure in its claims for love. They earlier decided on marriage and children, Percy's virtues. This human love is full and secure.

Section 12 begins, "Father Weatherbee sat behind Jack Curl's
mahogany desk with its collection of Russian ikons and bleeding
Mexican crucifixes" (*SC,* 356). As Will attempts to persuade the
reticent old man to perform the marriage ceremony, the narrative
concentrates on his age, physical deterioration, and general use-
lessness as he attempts to avoid whatever the priestly Jack Curl
would do. Will stupidly urges him as he once did Sutter to reveal
the secret, making a reservation: "We are also willing to take in-
structions, as long as you recognize I cannot and will not accept all
of your dogmas. Unless of course you have the authority to tell me
something I don't know. Do you?" (*SC,* 358). Will is even willing
to have the priest declare his own authority, without demanding
proof. The apostle in whatever unlikely form has divine authority,
though this physically unpresumptive old minister supports the
doctrine of Apostolic Succession, which means that he is claiming
precisely to have an authority conferred through charge and touch
from St. Peter himself as head of the earthly church.

When the priest at last speaks, he tells of the poor villagers in
Mindanao: " 'They believed me! They believed the Gospel whole
and entire, and the teachings of the church. They said that if I told
them, then it must be true or I would not have gone to so much
trouble' " (*SC,* 359). So Father Weatherbee answers Will. He is
spreading the Gospel. He is authorized. Here is Will's truth, as
well as his one and only answer to all the questions he has put
during his lifetime to all those he temporarily considered authorities.
But with all his sophistication, Will is not well. His Ph is awry—
and he worries that he will miss the signs of the second coming.
"What do I want of him, mused Will Barrett. . . . Will Barrett
thought about Allie in her greenhouse, her wide gray eyes, her lean
muscled boy's arms, her strong quick hands. His heart leapt with
a secret joy. What is it I want from her and him, he wondered,
not only want but must have? Is she a gift and therefore a sign of
a giver? Could it be that the Lord is here, masquerading behind
this simple silly holy face? Am I crazy to want both, her and Him?
No, not want, must have. And will have" (*SC,* 360).

These beautiful, simple words end the novel and what may be
Percy's work. Binx, a character so apparently different from Will,
long ago made a question that was a suggestion: "Or is it because
he believes that God himself is present here at the corner of Elysian
Fields and Bon Enfants? . . . through some dim dazzling trick of

grace, coming for the one and receiving the other as God's own importunate bonus?" (*M*, 235). Tom said, "It is Christmas Day and the Lord is here, a holy night and surely that is all one needs" (*LR*, 402).

The unity Percy attempts to show in this last scene illustrates remarks he makes in the self-interview quoted above: "Life is a mystery, love is a delight. Therefore I take it as axiomatic that one should settle for nothing less than the infinite mystery and the infinite delight, i. e., God. In fact I demand It. I refuse to settle for anything less" (p. 190). So Will takes this woman not as Lancelot took Margot, as substitute for God, but as gift from God.

Chapter Ten
Meanwhile

All of Walker Percy's novels are about love: human love and divine love. They are human love stories at the center of which a man and a woman are married or propose to marry with a new beginning in prospect. This prospective marriage values the old virtues. First the marriage itself is important. Fidelity is assumed and sexual license literally deplored. Children are expected and desired, despite the several suffering children mentioned in the various novels. In *The Second Coming,* Will explicitly speaks of the idea of having children after all the mistreatment both he and Allison have endured and after he has himself made a reservation somewhat earlier. He considers, like Binx and Tom if not Lance directly, forming a Christian home. And herein is the foundation for that other love, the divine. It becomes a man to indulge his sexual propensities only as a miracle illustrating the ways of God to man and not as either a mindless or a hubristic function of his own mortal being.

Percy has in the essays made a good deal of the theological and philosophical aspects of his thinking—recovery of being. But his novels, and his essays overall, are at times subtle, and at times reiterative, edifying discourses urging the main Roman Catholic doctrines about faith, good works, marriage, and family. Against these he displays human failures in sex and religion—indiscriminate search for pleasure and enslavement of blacks. Sex and religion—involving the first two commandments, really. Loving sex is failure to love God, in allowing an essential human capacity to contravene the relationship that man might have with God. This observation has to do with the first commandment. For the second, the idea is that mistreatment of others is failure to respect others as beings.

Given the virtues—the faith in God and at least the general rightmindedness about ethical conduct—the question is still what to do with a lifetime. If they are lucky, Will and Allison will be together companionably at four o'clock on any dull afternoon, a crucial time in Percy's view because it tests the joy of living *all* the time, when superficial or temporary excitement no longer satisfies. And they have plans for a long future. Their intent, recovery of being, is a devotion, nearly a vocation, actually to live, to participate in human activity with each other, as celebrants of being.

Percy, that is, has repeatedly questioned what to do with the here and now. What about the interim before the second coming? What is the purpose of human being as a condition that negates nonbeing? How, in short, is a human being to spend the time of his life in living? The answer is to have faith and to practice morality in something like the traditional manner, by loving family and friends. And with a theme found in all his novels, he suggests what the occupation of mankind should be. It begins in *The Moviegoer* with an abrupt passage.

The passage ends Binx's account of his estrangement from Walter, a college friend, and from other friends whom he left in the midst of a trek along the Appalachian Trail to " 'go back to New Orleans and live in Gentilly.' " He continues in the next sentence, "And there I have lived ever since, solitary and in wonder, wondering day and night, never a moment without wonder. . . . and not for five minutes will I be distracted from the wonder" (*M*, 41–42).

Lewis Lawson says Binx is referring to what Sartre calls fascination. "All that he can establish is that he is not the object that fascinates him, the world, so he lives in Sartre's state of 'fascination.' " Lawson quotes Sartre as saying, "the condition necessary for the existence of fascination is that the object be raised in absolute relief on a background of emptiness; that is, I am precisely the immediate negation of the object and nothing but that."[1] This condition explains the move to Gentilly, an intellectual desert where Binx reads only *Arabia Deserta* and a clipping from *Reader's Digest,* away from cultured and indulgent New Orleans. And it is the desert place where Binx begins his search as well as where he begins to see the world with the school playground, the sky, and the clouds.

This wonder is associated with a twofold concept often found in Percy's novels—watching and waiting. Later, Binx says he awoke during the night and lay "dozing yet wakeful and watchful" (*M*, 83), a situation that hints of portent. He also speaks of what he calls an "immense curiosity" felt when he woke on the battlefield and saw the dung beetle. This experience and this emotion are somehow related to the mundane but wondrous situation he has on the morning of the narrative beginning. He sees the items on the dresser, his "belongings," which "looked both familiar and at the same time full of clues" (*M*, 11). And some time before while watching *Red River*, he felt "the first faint stirrings of curiosity about the particular seat I was in" (*M*, 75).

Ever since he had an experience of unconsciousness in the army, he says, he is wakeful, asking himself, "What is this that is going to happen? Clearly nothing. Yet there I lie, wakeful and watchful as a sentry . . ." (*M*, 84). Later, he says, "Instead of trying to sleep I try to fathom the mystery of this suburb at dawn" (*M*, 86). Seeing another Western movie that reminds him of seeing *The Oxbow Incident* years before again makes him "wonder about the enduring, about all the nights, the rainy summer nights at twelve and one and two o'clock when the seats endured alone in the empty theater. The enduring is something which must be accounted for. One cannot simply shrug it off " (*M*, 80).

The wonder mentioned here is related closely to the search, even if the connection is hardly made in the novel. Binx says, "The search is what anyone would undertake if he were not sunk in the everydayness of his own life. This morning, for example, I felt as if I had come to myself on a strange island. And what does such a castaway do? Why, he pokes around the neighborhood and he doesn't miss a trick" (*M*, 13). This experience is living and learning mystery within one's own immediate environment, a situation discussed in "The Message in the Bottle." For Binx, Gentilly and the Garden District; for man, the environment and the realm of mystery are the universe. Or as the narrator says in *The Second Coming*, this is a "world of endless wonders" (*SC*, 189), where man lives and has his being.

The immense curiosity is more elaborately developed in *Lancelot* than elsewhere. Lancelot's entire narrative and his entire experience derive from his curiosity: "Then it was that the worm of interest burned somewhere near the base of my spine. Curious. What was curious?" (*L*, 27). His one slight insignificant worm of interest turns him out of his daily ritual of ordinariness and leads to a consideration of life and all its meaning. Though he first suffers then murders, he also lives. The novel is a narrative of events following from this quickening experience.

In *The Last Gentleman*, as Will attempts to show his sympathy with the young black, he urges David not to become a sportscaster.

" 'What I'm going to do!' cried David.
" 'Do like me,' said the engineer seriously. 'Watch and wait. Keep your
  eyes open.' " (*LG*, 226)

Will is serious because that has been his occupation, having found
himself, like Binx, the last of a line of declining activists.

So living for him was a strain. . . . So he became a watcher and a listener
and a wanderer. He could not get enough of watching. Once when he
was a boy, a man next door had gone crazy and had sat out in his back
yard pitching gravel around and hollering out to his enemies in a loud
angry voice. The boy watched him all day, squatted down and watched
him, his mouth open and drying. It seemed to him that if he could figure
out what was wrong with the man he would learn the great secret of life.
(*LG*, 10)

(Tom has a somewhat less intriguing encounter with the golf pro
in *Love in the Ruins*.)
    Perhaps *Love in the Ruins* makes the most use of this concept.
Tom says in the epilogue, "Five Years Later," that "Here's one
difference between this age and the last. Now while you work, you
also watch and listen and wait. . . . If you want and work and
wait, you can have. . . . Poor as I am, I feel like God's spoiled
child. I am Robinson Crusoe set down on the best possible island
with a library, a laboratory, a lusty Presbyterian wife, a cozy tree
house, an idea, and all the time in the world" (*LR*, 381–83). And
in a passage that purposely breaks off in the midst of an idea about
the second coming, Tom says, "what with the spirit of the new age
being the spirit of watching and waiting" (*LR*, 387). A "serene
watchfulness" is what Tom urges after his long journey through
hell and purgatory.
    As noted above, Lancelot begins a process of watching and waiting
when he notices the minor "error" on the medical certificate about
Siobhan's blood type. He says that overnight he became "alert,
watchful as a tiger at a water hole" (*L*, 140). And in the scene of
the young man in the Shenandoah Valley: "All one can say for
certain is that he is watching and waiting" (*L*, 221). Later, Lance
broadens views in the attempt to explain partly what has happened.
On discovering Margot's infidelity, he discovered his freedom, he
says. And he compares himself to another who opened eyes on the
new world: "it was as if I had been wakened from a twenty-year

dream. I was Rip van Winkle rubbing his eyes. In an instant I became sober, alert, watchful. I could act" (*L,* 107). This may be the first time anyone has said *act* in Percy's work, but this state of release is characteristic of Percy's main characters.

Autobiography is the ultimate source of all this interest in watching and waiting. Percy says (in his essay about life with "Uncle Will") that he was himself "a youth whose only talent was a knack for looking and listening, for tuning in and soaking up."[2] In discussing his theories about art (significantly called "From Facts to Fiction"), Percy says that in writing *The Moviegoer* he thought of a character like Crusoe waking on his island filled with wonder and curiosity.[3] Crusoe is a favorite symbol for Percy, used also to elucidate his theories of epistemology. Rather than having knowledge packaged and handed on from teacher to pupil in a formal situation, Percy encourages direct encounters between students and objects, man and the world, individual existence itself, as primal being and the opposite of nonexistence. From this urge comes the observation from Binx that he will study the "mystery which surrounds him" (*M,* 52) and Will's about the "singularity of things" (*LG,* 188). Percy thinks that Crusoe was eminently revealing the value of this approach to learning and to living in the world. It means that the individual lives his life as if he were the only person—the first person—in a newly made universe, encountering the miraculous world itself for the first time, all quite as if being and miracle depended on him alone. Yet of course it does not. He watches and waits from ulterior intent, admonished to do so in the good news brought as a singular kind of divine truth from God himself: "Watch ye therefore and also wait. For ye know not the day and the hour wherein the son of man cometh." All this is for God's sake. Yet, as Binx says, finally, for good and selfish reasons—one's salvation.

Notes and References

Chapter One

1. See " 'Uncle Will' and His South," *Saturday Review/World* 1 (November 6, 1973):22–25 and introduction to *Lanterns on the Levee: Recollections of a Planter's Son*, by William Alexander Percy (Baton Rouge, 1973).
2. John Carr, "An Interview with Walker Percy," *Georgia Review* 25 (Fall 1971):317.
3. Walker Percy, "From Facts to Fiction," *Book Week* 4 (December 25, 1966); reprinted in *The Writer*, October 1967, pp. 27–28, 46. This item narrates the experience of his illness, discusses his reading and accounts for his shift from science to art.
4. Percy, "Uncle Will," p. 22. The next quotation is from page 24.
5. Martin Luschei, *The Sovereign Wayfarer: Walker Percy's Diagnosis of the Malaise* (Baton Rouge, 1972), p. 17.
6. Walker Percy, "Questions They Never Asked Me," *Esquire* 88 (December 1977):193–94.
7. Walker Percy, "Random Thoughts on Southern Literature, Southern Politics, and the American Future," *Georgia Review* 32 (Fall 1978):499–511.
8. Walker Percy, "Virtues and Vices in the Southern Literary Renascence," *Commonwealth* 76 (May 11, 1962):182.
9. Walker Percy, "Mississippi: The Fallen Paradise," *Harper's Magazine* 230 (April 1965):172.
10. Carlton Cremeens, "Walker Percy, The Man and the Novelist: An Interview," *Southern Review*, n.s. 4 (Spring 1968):284.
11. He wrote three articles published in 1935, one called "The Movie Magazine: A Low 'Slick,' " *Carolina Magazine* 64 (March 1935):4–9.
12. See Luschei's biography for details of his revisions.
13. Bradley R. Dewey, "Walker Percy Talks about Kierkegaard: An Annotated Interview," *Journal of Religion* 54 (July 1974):288.
14. Dewey, p. 291.
15. On this Kierkegaardian influence, see Luschei, passim. Sometimes this influence seems permanent and pervasive.
16. Herbert Mitgang, "A Talk with Walker Percy," *New York Times Book Review*, February 20, 1977, p. 1.

17. Zoltán Abádi-Nagy, "A Talk with Walker Percy," *Southern Literary Journal* 6 (Fall 1973):7.

18. See John Saward, *Perfect Fools: Folly for Christ's Sake in Catholic and Orthodox Spirituality* (Oxford: Oxford University Press, 1980), passim.

19. Walker Percy, "The Coming Crisis in Psychiatry," *America* 96 (January 12, 1957):415.

20. Ibid., p. 418.

21. See Jared W. Bradley, "Walker Percy and the Search for Wisdom," *Louisiana Studies* 12 (1973):581.

Chapter Two

1. Barbara King, "Walker Percy Prevails," *Southern Voices,* May–June 1974, p. 23.

2. Carr, p. 325.

3. Abádi-Nagy, p. 12.

4. Carr, p. 326.

5. King, p. 20.

6. Cremeens, pp. 273–74.

7. Carr, p. 318.

8. Walker Percy," The State of the Novel: Dying Art or New Science?" *Michigan Quarterly Review* 16 (Fall 1977):363.

9. Ibid., p. 372.

10. Walker Percy, "Naming and Being," *Personalist* 41 (Spring 1960):156.

11. Cremeens, p. 279.

12. Ibid., p. 282.

13. Carr, p. 321.

14. Ibid., p. 322.

15. "A Symposium on Fiction: Donald Barthelme, William Gass, Grace Paley, Walker Percy," *Shenandoah* 27 (Winter 1976):12, 4, 6.

16. Cremeens, p. 280.

17. Bruce Cook, "New Faces in Faulkner Country," *Saturday Review* 3 (September 4, 1976):41.

18. Cremeens, p. 275.

19. Percy, "From Facts to Fiction," p. 9.

20. Cremeens, p. 280.

21. King, p. 23.

22. Cremeens, p. 281.

23. [Marcus Smith], "Talking about Talking: An Interview with Walker Percy," *New Orleans Review* 5, no. 1 (1976):17.

24. Smith, p. 16.

25. "Symposium," p. 23.

26. See Charles P. Bigger, "Walker Percy and the Resonance of the Word," *Southern Quarterly* 18 (Spring 1980):43–54.
27. Paul L. Gaston, *Journal of Modern Literature* 5, no. 4 (1976):612.
28. Panthea Reid Broughton, "A Bottle Unopened, A Message Unread," *Virginia Quarterly Review* 52 (Winter 1975):973.
29. Walter Michaels, *Georgia Review* 29 (Winter 1975):973.
30. Percy, "Random Thoughts," p. 504.
31. Carr, p. 331.
32. Percy, "Random Thoughts," p. 509.
33. Walker Percy, "The Left Hand of Sheed," *America* 128 (May 12, 1973):439. See also Abádi-Nagy, p. 11.
34. John Gardner, "The Quest for the Philosophical Novel," *New York Times Book Review,* February 20, 1977, p. 20.
35. Percy, "Questions They Never Asked Me," p. 172.

Chapter Three

1. Dewey, p. 291.
2. Percy, "Virtues and Vices," p. 182.
3. Cremeens, p. 272.
4. Ibid., p. 272. Percy's essays dealing with civil rights include "The Failure and the Hope," "Red, White and Blue-Gray," "Mississippi: The Fallen Paradise," "A Southern View," "The Southern Moderate," and "Random Thoughts," all in the bibliography.
5. Ibid., p. 276.
6. Ibid.
7. Abádi-Nagy, p. 18.
8. Percy, "Random Thoughts," p. 502.
9. Ibid., p. 503.
10. Percy, "Questions They Never Asked Me," pp. 188, 190.
11. Carr, p. 332.
12. This phrase generally belongs to Panthea Reid Broughton, "Gentlemen and Fornicators: *The Last Gentleman* and a Bisected Reality," in *The Art of Walker Percy: Stratagems for Being,* ed. Panthea Reid Broughton (Baton Rouge, 1979), pp. 96–114.

Chapter Four

1. Abádi-Nagy, p. 16.
2. William Dowie, "Walker Percy, Sensualist-Thinker," *Novel* 6 (1972), p. 53.
3. Dewey, p. 294.
4. James Dickey, *American Scholar* 37 (Summer 1968), p. 524. Percy likes to take lines and words or phrases from other writers. T. S. Eliot, with his sexual wasteland and hurrying time, is obvious. Gerard Manley

Hopkins supplies words: "pied," "dappled," "gear, tackle, trim" (LR, 309). Dante is paraphrased at the beginning of Lost in the Ruins, and later the beautiful line from Dante's tale of Paolo and Francesca is applied to Alistair and Doris: "And that day we read no more." Will's use of "old mole" to refer to his father in The Second Coming is presumably from Hamlet's use of the term (once). One of the most charming borrowings is from William (Johnson) Cory's translation of Callimachus, which Aunt Emily paraphrases. The original is "I wept as I remembered how often you and I / Had tired the sun with talking and sent him down the sky." Several others appear in various works.

    5. Abádi-Nagy, pp. 10–11.

Chapter Five

    1. Ashley Brown, "An Interview with Walker Percy," *Shenandoah* 18 (Spring 1967):7.
    2. Judith Serebnick, "First Novelists—Spring 1961," *Library Journal* 86 (February 1, 1961):597.
    3. Abádi-Nagy, p. 4.
    4. Dewey, p. 284.
    5. For a list of important discussions of moviegoing, see Lewis Lawson, "Moviegoing in *The Moviegoer*," *Southern Quarterly* 18 (Spring 1980):26–42 passim and n. 1.
    6. Jim Van Cleave, "Versions of Percy," *Southern Review*, n.s. 6 (1970):990–1010.
    7. Abádi-Nagy, p. 6.
    8. Ibid., p. 15.
    9. Carr, p. 329.
    10. Ibid., p. 327.
    11. Percy discusses the stoic virtues in "Mississippi," pp. 166–72.

Chapter Six

    1. Carr, p. 328.
    2. Brown, p. 7.
    3. Abádi-Nagy, p. 16.
    4. Cremeens, p. 285.
    5. Abádi-Nagy, p. 12.
    6. Carr, p. 329.

Chapter Seven

    1. Abádi-Nagy, p. 17.
    2. Ibid., p. 16.
    3. Ibid., p. 6.

Chapter Eight

1. John F. Baker, "PW Interviews: Walker Percy," *Publishers' Weekly* 211 (March 21, 1977):6.
2. Mitgang, p. 20.
3. Use of a relatively colorless *unspeakable* with such specificity, insistence and repetition may indicate the influence of Wittgenstein and other philosophers (such as Kant) regarding those metaphysical or transcendental matters simply beyond human perception and description. See Allan Janik and Stephen Toulmin, *Wittgenstein's Vienna* (New York: Simon and Schuster, 1973), p. 233.

Chapter Nine

1. Eric Voegelin, *The Ecumenic Age* (Baton Rouge: Louisiana State University Press, 1974), p. 73. For existentialists, a prospective event might be more immediate than an event in the chronological present.

Chapter Ten

1. Lawson, p. 28.
2. Percy, " 'Uncle Will' and His South," p. 22.
3. Percy, "From Facts to Fiction," p. 9. In *The Philosophy of History,* G.W.F. Hegel (antagonist to Kierkegaard and by implication to Percy) has a fascinating comment on Greek wonder "at the *Natural* in Nature" (New York: Dover Publications, 1956), p. 234.

Selected Bibliography

Compiled and annotated by Joe Weixlmann (Indiana State University)

It has been possible to list here only the more important and/or representative writings by and about Walker Percy. Those seeking references to lesser Percy-related works should consult Joe Weixlmann and Daniel H. Gann, "Walker Percy Bibliography," *Southern Quarterly* 18, no. 3 (1980):137–57.

PRIMARY SOURCES

1. Books

Lancelot. New York: Farrar, Straus and Giroux, 1977.

The Last Gentleman. New York: Farrar, Straus and Giroux, 1966.

Love in the Ruins: The Adventures of a Bad Catholic at a Time Near the End of the World. New York: Farrar, Straus and Giroux, 1971.

The Message in the Bottle: How Queer Man Is, How Queer Language Is, and What One Has to Do with the Other. New York: Farrar, Straus and Giroux, 1975. Includes "The Delta Factor" (1975), "The Loss of the Creature" (1958), "Metaphor as Mistake" (1958), "The Man on the Train: Three Existential Modes" (1956), "Notes for a Novel about The End of the World" (1967–68), "The Message in the Bottle" (1959), "The Mystery of Language" (1957), "Toward a Triadic Theory of Meaning" (1972), "The Symbolic Structure of Interpersonal Process" (1961), "Culture: The Antinomy of the Scientific Method" (1958), "Semiotic and a Theory of Knowledge" (1957), "Symbol, Consciousness, and Intersubjectivity" (1958), "Symbol as Hermeneutic in Existentialism" (1956), "Symbol as Need" (1954), "A Theory of Language" (1975).

The Moviegoer. New York: Alfred A. Knopf, 1961.

The Second Coming. New York: Farrar, Straus and Giroux, 1980.

2. Uncollected Essays (arranged chronologically)

"Stoicism in the South." *Commonweal* 64 (July 6, 1956):342–44.

"The Coming Crisis in Psychiatry." *America* 96 (January 5, 1957):391–93; 96 (January 12, 1957):415–18.
"A Southern View." *America* 97 (July 20, 1957):428–29.
"The Southern Moderate." *Commonweal* 67 (December 13, 1957):279–82.
"The Culture Critics." *Commonweal* 70 (June 5, 1959):247–50.
"Naming and Being." *Personalist* 41 (Spring 1960):148–57.
"Red, White, and Blue-Gray." *Commonweal* 75 (December 22, 1961):337–39.
"Mississippi: The Fallen Paradise." *Harper's Magazine* 230 (April 1965):166–72.
"The Failure and the Hope." *Katallagete* 1 (December 1965):16–21.
"From Facts to Fiction." *Book Week* 4 (December 25, 1966), 6, 9.
Introduction to *Lanterns on the Levee: Recollections of a Planter's Son,* by William Alexander Percy. Baton Rouge: Louisiana State University Press, 1973, pp. vii–xviii.
" 'Uncle Will' and His South." *Saturday Review/World* 1 (November 6, 1973):22–25.
"The State of the Novel: Dying Art or New Science?" *Michigan Quarterly Review* 16 (Fall 1977):359–73.
"Random Thoughts on Southern Literature, Southern Politics, and the American Future." *Georgia Review* 32 (Fall 1978):499–511.

SECONDARY SOURCES

1. Books and Articles

Bigger, Charles P. "Walker Percy and the Resonance of the Word." *Southern Quarterly* 18, no. 3 (1980):43–54. Avers that, while Percy, in *The Message in the Bottle,* "sometimes tends to traffic in dead issues and shun arguments which would make his case even more dazzling and his achievement more accessible," he "has performed a remarkable service towards our recovery of [a true sense of] strangeness" through his discussions of the mystery of naming.
Broughton, Panthea Reid. "Gentlemen and Fornicators: *The Last Gentleman* and a Bisected Reality." In *The Art of Walker Percy: Stratagems for Being,* edited by Panthea Reid Broughton. Baton Rouge: Louisiana State University Press, 1979, pp. 96–114, 306. Contends that one reason for Percy's art falling short of complete success is that Percy "uses sexual matters as convenient illustrations of Cartesian dualism" yet "fails to see in them a means for overcoming that split." At the end of *The Last Gentleman,* we find Percy "conceptualizing in terms of that very mind/body split he and his characters deplore."

Cheney, Brainard. "Secular Society as Deadly Farce." *Sewanee Review* 75 (1967):345–50. Elucidates Percy's use of farce, satire, and sexuality in *The Last Gentleman.*

Coles, Robert. *Walker Percy: An American Search.* Boston: Little, Brown, 1979. Surveys Percy's "philosophical roots," his essays, and his fiction through *Lancelot* but is more given to providing encomia than to offering fresh critical insights.

Dowie, William, S.J. "Walker Percy: Sensualist-Thinker." *Novel* 6 (1972):52–65. Asserts that central to the experience of Percy's protagonists is the attempt to hold in dynamic tension the opposing pulls of sensation and thought. "*Love in the Ruins* brings the struggle to greater resolution than either of the previous works."

Gaston, Paul L. "The Revelation of Walker Percy." *Colorado Quarterly* 20 (1972):459–70. Explores some of the autobiographical elements in *The Moviegoer, The Last Gentleman,* and especially *Love in the Ruins* and argues that Percy's settings, though specific, have broad implications: "The details . . . may be unfamiliar at first, but the important ones are just around our own corners."

Godshalk, W. L. "Walker Percy's Christian Vision." *Louisiana Studies* 13 (1974):130–41. Attempts to demonstrate that "the main themes in *Love in the Ruins* underline that Percy is much more the Christian thinker than the existentialist philosopher, and our vision of his fiction is sharpened when we acknowledge this fact."

Hardy, John Edward. "Percy and Place: Some Beginnings and Endings." *Southern Quarterly* 18, no. 3 (1980):5–25. Uses Percy's initial scenic descriptions in *The Moviegoer, The Last Gentleman, Love in the Ruins,* and *Lancelot* as a catalyst for some refreshing critical observations about the books' protagonists—and their endings.

Johnson, Mark. "The Search for Place in Walker Percy's Novels." *Southern Literary Journal* 8, no. 1 (1975):55–81. Notes Percy's "remarkable concern for places" in *The Moviegoer, The Last Gentleman,* and *Love in the Ruins* and argues that these places perform three (sometimes overlapping) functions: They serve as vehicles for Percy's philosophy, as "illustrations of artificial as opposed to authentic environments," and as metaphorical representations of both the protagonist's mode of existence and the condition of his society. With each successive novel, Percy's sense of place "is more fully realized and enriches the novel accordingly."

Kennedy, J. Gerald. "The Sundered Self and the Riven World: *Love in the Ruins.*" In *The Art of Walker Percy: Strategems for Being,* edited by Panthea Reid Broughton. Baton Rouge: Louisiana State University Press, 1979, pp. 115–36, 306–7. Uses *Love in the Ruins* to illustrate his contention that Percy's use of Cartesian dualism may enable the novelist to investigate relationships "in clinical fashion," but "it leads likewise to an oversimplification of human personality."

Kissel, Susan S. "Walker Percy's 'Conversions.'" *Southern Literary Journal* 9, no. 2 (1977):124–36. Maintains that the protagonists of *The Moviegoer, The Last Gentleman,* and *Love in the Ruins* "undergo radical 'conversions' in their lives" at the conclusion of each novel, adopting an "unassuming, but not despairing" viewpoint and changing their goals, attitudes, and assumptions about man's purpose on earth.

Lawson, Lewis A. "The Gnostic Vision in *Lancelot.*" *Renascence* 32 (1979):52–64. Argues that Gnosticism, especially as it has been explained by Eric Voegelin in *The New Science of Politics,* resides at the core of *Lancelot.* As long as Lance Lamar finds sustenance in his Gnostic "vision" and rejects the orthodox Christianity of Father John, asserts Lawson, "there can be no hope for him."

———. "Moviegoing in *The Moviegoer.*" *Southern Quarterly* 18, no. 3 (1980):26–42. Offers a detailed examination of moviegoing as the thematic center of *The Moviegoer* and Percy's primary vehicle for dramatizing the novel's existential premises.

———. "Walker Percy's Indirect Communications." *Texas Studies in Literature and Language* 11 (1969):867–900. Carefully explores the roots and implications of Percy's theological thought and expression, especially as they evidence the influence of Kierkegaard. Lawson maintains that, unlike Percy's essays or "direct communications," *The Moviegoer* and *The Last Gentleman* communicate important religious issues indirectly, catching smug readers through aesthetics and then— via dramatization and wit—covertly attacking their religious illusions.

———. "Walker Percy's Silent Character." *Mississippi Quarterly* 33 (1980):123–40. Investigates the narrative structure of *Lancelot,* focusing on the five-day "silent invitation" which Father John offers to Lance Lamar as the priest attempts to effect the protagonist's salvation.

LeClair, Thomas. "Death and Black Humor." *Critique* 17, no. 1 (1975):5–40. Uses *The Last Gentleman* to illustrate Percy's kinship with other contemporary practitioners of Black Humor, a mode "primarily funereal."

———. "The Eschatological Vision of Walker Percy." *Renascence* 26 (1974):115–22. Focusing on *Love in the Ruins,* but also considering *The Moviegoer* and *The Last Gentleman,* argues that Percy's use of paradox, inversion, and incongruity is consistent with the dual eschatological vision which operates in his fiction: the "immanent eschatology" implicit in the existential analysis of death as a condition of life and the "transcendent eschatology" which can be found in Percy's presentation of death as an "event in the economy of salvation."

————. "Walker Percy's Devil." *Southern Literary Journal* 10, no. 1 (1977):3–13. Describes the "aesthetic inconsistency" of *Love in the Ruins* by demonstrating that Percy's conventional handling of narrative form in the novel is at odds with the existential principles articulated in Percy's essays and interviews. *The Moviegoer*, in particular, is more true to the novelist's avowed aesthetics.

Lehan, Richard. "The Way Back: Redemption in the Novels of Walker Percy." *Southern Review*, n.s. 4 (1968):306–19. Uses the existential modes described in Percy's essay "The Man on the Train"—"alienation," "rotation" (moving from an I-It to an I-Thou relationship), and "return" (seeking to create a meaningful future by reexperiencing the past)—as a lens through which to explain the strengths and weaknesses of *The Moviegoer* and *The Last Gentleman*. Lehan concludes that Percy is "brilliant" when describing a character's sense of alienation and quite capable when handling the sense of dislocation that comes with rotation but that the novelist has yet to find the narrative means to make the return convincing.

Luschei, Martin. *The Sovereign Wayfarer: Walker Percy's Diagnosis of the Malaise*. Baton Rouge: Louisiana State University Press, 1972. Traces the influence of Kierkegaard and Marcel on Percy, defines some relevant philosphical concepts, and offers extended readings of *The Moviegoer*, *The Last Gentleman*, and *Love in the Ruins* in making a case for Percy's being an existentialist novelist whose "great achievement may prove to have been translating Kierkegaard into concrete American terms."

Pearson, Michael. "Art as Symbolic Action: Walker Percy's Aesthetic." *Southern Quarterly* 18, no. 3 (1980):55–64. Suggests that Percy's language philosophy offers a key to unlocking his belief in the intersubjectivity of literature and contends that *Lancelot* evidences the novelist's clearest attempt to create an intersubjective moment in which the reader must take (symbolic) action by turning speaker— or accept the implications of the final silence.

Poteat, William H. "Reflections on Walker Percy's Theory of Language." In *The Art of Walker Percy: Strategems for Being*, edited by Panthea Reid Broughton. Baton Rouge: Louisiana State University Press, 1979, pp. 192–218, 308–9. Argues that *The Message in the Bottle* is "an edifying and *profound* failure" in which Percy tends to betray his deepest and most true philosophical insights "when he undertakes to give them explicit embodiment in the medium of an essay." When Percy allows his intuition to take control, as he does in "The Delta Factor," he is on more stable ground than he is when offering conceptual formulations.

Vauthier, Simone. "Title as Microtext: The Example of *The Moviegoer.*" *Journal of Narrative Technique* 5 (1975):219–29. Provides some new inroads into *The Moviegoer* while explaining the appropriateness of the novel's title.

Zeugner, John F. "Walker Percy and Gabriel Marcel: The Castaway and the Wayfarer." *Mississippi Quarterly* 28 (1974–75):21–53. Observes that, whereas Percy, in *The Moviegoer,* evidences a clear understanding of the thought of the influential philosopher Gabriel Marcel, *The Last Gentleman* and *Love in the Ruins* lack the delicate ideological balance found in Percy's first novel. Political considerations have removed the edge from the novelist's finely honed phenomenology; snobbery and smugness have surfaced and, in the process, caused his well-wrought irony to vanish.

2. Interviews and Panel Discussions

Abádi-Nagy, Zoltán. "A Talk with Walker Percy." *Southern Literary Journal* 6 (Fall 1973):3–19.

Brown, Ashley. "An Interview with Walker Percy." *Shenandoah* 18 (Spring 1967):3–10.

Carr, John. "An Interview with Walker Percy." *Georgia Review* 25 (Fall 1971):317–32.

Cremeens, Carlton. "Walker Percy, The Man and the Novelist: An Interview." *Southern Review,* n.s. 4 (Spring 1968):271–90.

Dewey, Bradley R. "Walker Percy Talks about Kierkegaard: An Annotated Interview." *Journal of Religion* 54 (July 1974):273–98.

King, Barbara. "Walker Percy Prevails." *Southern Voices* 1 (May–June 1974):19–23.

Mitgang, Herbert. "A Talk with Walker Percy." *New York Times Book Review,* February 20, 1977, pp. 1, 20–21.

Percy, Walker. "Questions They Never Asked Me." *Esquire* 88 (December 1977):170, 172, 184, 186, 188, 190, 193–94.

[**Smith, Marcus.**] "Talking about Talking: An Interview with Walker Percy." *New Orleans Review* 5, no. 1 (1976):13–18.

"A Symposium on Fiction: Donald Barthelme, William Gass, Grace Paley, Walker Percy." *Shenandoah* 27 (Winter 1976):3–31.

Index